PENGUIN BOOKS

REVOLUTION X

Rob Nelson and Jon Cowan are the co-founders of Lead . . . or Leave, the largest Generation X political organization in the United States, and a leading force in the effort to put generational issues on the national political map. Since launching Lead . . . or Leave in August of 1992, Jon and Rob have worked to educate and energize tens of thousands of younger Americans in the fight for a more sustainable economic, social, and environmental future. Lead . . . or Leave has chapters in all 50 states and an active Internet forum called ActioNet. They are reachable at (800) 44-CHANGE or lol @ mit.edu.

A SURVIVAL GUIDE

REVOLUTION X

FOR OUR GENERATION

ROB NELSON ■ JON COWAN
CO-FOUNDERS, LEAD . . . OR LEAVE

PENGUIN BOOKS

PENGUIN BOOKS
Published by the Penguin Group
Penguin Books USA Inc., 375 Hudson Street,
New York, New York 10014, U.S.A.
Penguin Books Ltd, 27 Wrights Lane,
London W8 5TZ, England
Penguin Books Australia Ltd, Ringwood,
Victoria, Australia
Penguin Books Canada Ltd, 10 Alcorn Avenue,
Toronto, Ontario, Canada M4V 3B2
Penguin Books (N.Z.) Ltd, 182–190 Wairau Road,
Auckland 10, New Zealand

Penguin Books Ltd, Registered Offices:
Harmondsworth, Middlesex, England

First published in Penguin Books 1994

1   3   5   7   9   10   8   6   4   2

LIBRARY OF CONGRESS CATALOGING IN PUBLICATION DATA
Nelson, Rob.
Revolution X: a survival guide for our generation/
Rob Nelson, Jon Cowan.
p. cm.
ISBN 0 14 02.3532 9
1. Political participation—United States.   2. Young adults—
United States—Political activity.   3. United States—Politics
and government—1993–   I. Cowan, Jon.   II. Title.
JK1764.N45   1994
323´.042´0973—dc20   94-15562

Printed in the United States of America
Set in Sabon

We dedicate this book to the millions in our generation who are tired of being put in a box and labeled, and who want to join the movement for a better future.

*Let no one be dismayed by the thought that
there is nothing that one man or woman
can do against the enormous array of the
world's ills.*

*Few will have the greatness to bend history
itself. But each can do some small act, and in
the sum of these events will be written the
history of our generation.*

—Senator Robert F. Kennedy, 1965

CONTENTS

GET IN THE GAME

A Foreword by Senator Bill Bradley

As a former NBA player, I know what happens when you sit on the sidelines. You can't move the ball. You don't score any points.

It's no different when it comes to winning a better future for you and your country. Democracy is not a spectator sport. Maybe you feel convinced that most of Washington cares more about reelection day than your future, but as *Revolution X* points out, that won't change unless you get in the game. You can't change the future from the sidelines.

There has never been a greater need for young America to get involved. We once thought it was our American birthright for our children to have a better standard of living than we do, but for the first time in history, that is no longer going to be the case. That is why your participation is so critical.

And participation begins with voting. Don't let Washington decide your future without your consent. There are more than 50 million eligible voters in your generation, yet fewer than half of you are reigstered to vote. We cannot act for you, we cannot speak for you, we cannot hear you when you are silent.

Whatever you do, whatever you believe, your generation is bound by some common goals: a sustainable economy, a healthy planet, and high-quality education.

Everyone in your generation loses if we just keep spending you and your future deeper into debt. The national debt is already large enough to pay Shaquille O'Neal's salary for over one and a half million years. Every one of you will pay the price if we don't start investing more in education, job training, and job creation. Right now, one in four kids lives in poverty, and half a million new college graduates each year can't find jobs. And all Americans—of all ages—will lose if we can't figure out a way to make health care affordable, to put more kids in school instead of in prison, and to ensure that the standard of living doesn't continue to drop.

Revolution X is a provocative book that makes a lot of assertions you can agree or disagree with. But no one can quarrel with the bottom line: You have to get involved.

The ball is in your court, and your future really is in your hands. *Revolution X* can help you play better, but each of you must first decide to get in the game.

INTRODUCTION: UNPLUGGED

OCTOBER 19, 1992: Several hundred younger Americans—students, professionals, waiters, bike messengers, even a congressional staffer—gathered on Capitol Hill in Washington to ask our national leaders to stop destroying our economic future.

A dozen of them went to talk with Senator Wyche Fowler, a first-term senator from Georgia. In the meeting, they urged the senator to show some accountability to coming generations and to make a pledge to cut the budget deficit—a pledge his opponent in the upcoming election had already made a few weeks earlier.

Fowler was not making any promises. Abruptly dismissing his audience, the senator stood up, stared at the young volunteers, and blurted out, "Students don't vote. Do you expect me to come in here and just kiss your ass?"

Newsweek ran the story in its next issue, and soon the senator's rude remarks were known across the country. Down in Georgia, younger voters attended Fowler rallies, holding up signs with their response: "Hey Wyche, students do vote. Kiss *our* ass!"

SITTING ON THE SIDELINES

Fowler lost his reelection bid by just 1 percent of the total vote. Looking back, it seems easy to dismiss Senator Fowler and his arrogance. After all, he was booted out of office.

But in a way, Senator Fowler's rebuke hits home. Millions of people in our generation don't get involved. We don't vote. We don't take a stand for our future. We don't get in the face of politicians to demand change.

Instead, we sit on the sidelines of our democracy, watching our taxes, crime rates, and tuition costs go up, while our quality of life, the value of our education, the health of our environment, and our chances of finding stable, high-paying jobs go down.

During our travels across the country, we have met and spoken with thousands of younger Americans—rich and poor, gay and straight, white, black, Hispanic, and Asian. We have held rallies in dozens of cities, organized students on hundreds of college and high school

campuses, and mobilized twenty- and thirtysomething professionals.

Almost everyone we spoke with, from rural
Kansas to Hollywood, California, agreed that
America was in trouble—and that they themselves would pay an enormously high price if
America didn't change its course soon. Yet very
few people, even those with money and fame,
thought that their individual contribution to
solving our national problems would make
much of a difference. That's no surprise. We're
a generation that was raised on images of politics and government gone sour: Vietnam,
Watergate, the $500 billion S&L scandal, and
Iran-Contra.

We've grown up listening day after day to
talking heads, career politicians, and endless
TV sound bites. Confused and frustrated, many
of us simply unplug and walk away. We look at
the biggest national problems—from homelessness to AIDS to the national debt—as too large
and complex to understand, much less fix.

But there's a high price for this generational
disconnectedness. In turning away from the
enormous challenges that face us, we are in
many ways forfeiting control over our individual destinies and over the collective fate of our
generation.

It doesn't have to be this way.

This book is for those of you who are tired
of feeling powerless and want to get involved in
shaping your future. It is written for those who

don't buy into the stereotype that "Generation
X" implies: a generation of apathetic, direc-
tionless youth who watch Beavis and Butt-
head, act like Bart Simpson, and drink Pepsi
because it's fun.

Most important, it is written for those who
want an end to the toxic policies that have been
dumped on our generation—and who are ready
to join in an effort to create a sustainable future
for all Americans, including those yet to come.

THE 13TH GENERATION

There are almost 80 million of us born between
1961 and 1981.

We are the 13th generation of Americans
since the founding of our country. We are the
most racially and socially diverse generation in
American history; yet despite the diversity that
sometimes divides us, many common experiences do unite us.

We are the first generation to talk by computer, the first to pass through metal detectors
to enter school, and the first to grow up on television.

We have the lowest job skills of any recent
group of Americans. We are the product of
more divorces and have a higher percentage in
prison than *any* generation before us.

We are also one of the most racially tolerant generations in U.S. history, we are privileged to live in a time of unprecedented medical miracles and a communications revolution that is redefining our country, and so far we have escaped the trauma of a protracted war.

Yet while many of us are grateful to live in America, we recognize and worry about the fact that our future has been sold out—put up for sale to the highest special-interest bidder.

Our political leaders have run up tremendous debts—economic, social, and environmental burdens that our generation and generations to come must confront. Now, on the edge of a new millennium, our generation has the difficult task of beginning the great American cleanup.

It's not that America's problems belong *only* to our generation. But we have come of age in a nation that is living on what it has borrowed from the future. That's a bill we—and those who follow us—will pay for the rest of our lives.

We grew up as America, in many ways, fell down.

While older generations watched Neil Armstrong plant an American flag on the moon, we tuned in to see Christa McAuliffe killed in the *Challenger* explosion. We are the first generation to come of age having safe sex and being forced to deal with a full-blown AIDS epidemic, the first to inherit a lower stan-

dard of living than our parents and a debt
that may soon eclipse the size of our economy.

LIVING GENERATIONS OF AMERICANS

Generation	Birth Years	Age in 1994
Lost Generation	1883–1900	94–111
G.I. Generation	1901–1924	70–93
Silent Generation	1925–1942	52–69
Boom Generation	1943–1960	34–51
Thirteenth Generation	**1961–1981**	**13–33**
Millennial Generation	1982–	12 and under

Source: *Generations*, Neil Howe and Bill Strauss.

Take a look at some of the foolish choices
Washington makes, and the impact they have
on *your* future:

■ *Each year Washington spends more on the
military than on education, making America
the only industrialized nation in the world
that continues to run such a spending imbal-
ance.* Yet the real battlefield is here at home,
where more than one in five children live in
poverty, our infant mortality rate is higher
than that of Singapore or South Korea, and a
young black man in Harlem is less likely to
live beyond the age of 45 than his counterpart
in Bangladesh is.

■ *We continue to allow U.S. factories to spew 3.4 billion pounds of toxic chemicals into America's air, land, and water a year.* That's despite having the highest level of air pollution in world history, a vanishing ozone layer, and a toxic cleanup bill that already tops three-quarters of a trillion dollars—half of one year's entire federal budget.

■ *In 1990, the federal government spent 11 times more per capita on senior citizens— overall the most affluent segment of the American population—than on children, the poorest part of the population.* For example, in 1991 the government gave $74 billion a year in Social Security and Medicare benefits to people with incomes over $50,000. Just one-third of that amount would fund a package of investments to protect the health and economic well-being of millions of children and save our generation hundreds of billions in future welfare and remedial education costs.

■ *Our Social Security system is so insecure that it will ultimately require a 40 percent tax hike on future generations to remain solvent.* The average Social Security recipient who retired in 1980 will get back everything he paid into the so-called "trust funds" in three years. Today's retirees will get it back in 10, rising to 18 years for someone retiring in 2030.

- *Our generation pays the highest relative taxes of any age group in America. Yet we get the fewest direct benefits.* And the situation is far worse for future generations, who can expect lifetime tax rates of 82 percent.

A CALL TO ACTION

We cannot easily undo decades of reckless leadership. But we can prevent it from further destroying America—and our future.

In the past 200 years, each generation of Americans has had its unique calling: breaking free of England, ending slavery, providing a safety net during the Great Depression, defeating the Nazis, gaining women's equality, and winning civil rights for millions.

Today, however, there is no easily identifiable enemy—no Hitler, King George, or Depression-era Dust Bowl. Today the enemy is us: a nation unwilling to stop living for the present at the expense of the future.

Perhaps older generations can afford to continue playing this game of chicken, seeing how much we can borrow from the future before we crash, but our generation has no such luxury. We're like Han Solo and Chewbacca in *Star Wars*: Either we make the leap into hyperspace or we're going to crash and burn.

Our generation's mission may seem less heroic than other battles, but it is just as vital:

We must lay aside our cynicism, get off our butts, and take a stand for our common future.

Do it for noble reasons or self-interested ones. Do it because you believe in America, or because you want a decent future. Do it if you've never volunteered anywhere or if you're already involved in politics. Do it to save your job, your student loan, your kid's future, or your own life.

But *do* it—because no one is coming to rescue our future, not our parents, grandparents, or political leaders. No one but us.

SURVIVING PAST THE 1990S

Revolution X is about empowering our generation and how a new and different approach to awareness and activism can help fix America.

The book begins with a look at the movement to reshape the country that's already started among younger Americans. Then it examines the harsh impact (and basic facts) of some of the largest crises facing our generation—including the exploding national debt, violent crime and poverty, and a hidden time bomb: the baby boomers' retirement early next century.

Finally, *Revolution X* lays out the tools you need to start gaining control over your future—including suggestions for personal and collective actions that do make a difference, and realistic, concrete solutions to some of the most difficult challenges facing our generation.

Although *Revolution X* draws on our experiences as full-time activists, neither of us were born believers in community and political action. Until the summer of 1992, we were as disillusioned as anyone we knew. We felt cut off from the people making decisions about our lives and frustrated by their choices. We did not see the power and potential of our generation to prevent our future from being destroyed.

Setting aside our doubts, we decided to take a risk and combined $1,000 from our own pockets to begin Lead . . . or Leave, a grass-roots campaign to give our generation a stronger voice in politics—and to make Washington stop selling out our future.

Today, Lead . . . or Leave is the largest non-partisan twentysomething political group in America, with a million members and chapters in every state.

Lead . . . or Leave has registered thousands of voters, educated millions about our economic and social crisis, organized hundreds of protests with people of all ages, and joined forces with many other groups, including Rock the Vote, United We Stand, the National Coalition for Student Empowerment, the Association of Big Ten Schools, the National Taxpayers Union, and the National Wildlife Federation.

But that is only the beginning.

Only when millions more of us get in the face of the system—read up and understand the crises we face, talk about them to friends and family, volunteer, vote, and speak our minds—only then will we see an end to the reckless policies that have mortgaged our future.

So the choice is yours: You are standing in the middle of the highway and a 50-ton truck is about to run you over. You can close your eyes and hope the truck misses—or you can do something, anything, to get out of the way.

CHAPTER ONE

REVOLUTION BY EVOLUTION

THESE ARE NOT the best of times. Most of us know this.

We see it in our McJobs, our shared living spaces, the declining value of our degrees, and our bank accounts that seem permanently empty.

We see it in the houses we can't afford, the health insurance we don't have, and the dreams we've already started to give up. We see it in our apathy and our anger, our music and our movies.

Rising incomes. Improved job prospects. The ability to own a home. Better living standards than your parents. A stronger economy than the previous generation. A safer world in which to raise your kids. Fewer of these promises will be fulfilled than at any time in our history. Most of us know this too.

> "The American Dream? Right now . . . the dream for me personally would just be to survive."
> —Kirsten, 24-year-old bartender

When surveyed, members of our generation say it will be harder for us to live as well as our parents. People for the American Way, a public-interest group, found that 68 percent of 15- to 24-year-olds thought that it was harder to be a young person today than when their parents were their age. Many believed America's best years were already gone.

A *Time* magazine/CNN survey reached the same conclusion when it conducted a poll of 18- to 29-year-old Americans. Sixty-five percent said it was going to be much harder to live as well as previous generations.

A generation of whiners? No—as we'll see in the coming chapters—a generation of realists. Every toxic policy that piles on more debt, destroys the environment, gives resources to the well-off instead of to those in economic need, or funds excessive military spending rather than addressing our social crisis jeopardizes the next generation's future.

By almost any standard—from access to affordable housing to quality of education, from employability to earning potentials to aggregate tax burdens—younger Americans are in trouble.

That's not just the Gospel According to Our Generation. John Chancellor, TV's elder statesman, described us as "the most invisible and possibly the most mistreated generation in American history. . . . More than any previous generation, these people deserve a bigger slice of [our national] pie."

DON'T CALL ME SLACKER

Despite the conventional wisdom that labels us a generation of slackers, brat-pack whiners who want it all for nothing (one study even called us a "generation of moral mutants"), a growing number in our generation are starting to fight back, and are looking for ways to make a difference.

- *More young people volunteer than at any time in the past 30 years.* Forty percent of all first-year college students partici- pated in some form of organized demonstration during 1992— more than double the number that did so in 1966 and 1967, during the Vietnam War and civil rights uprisings.

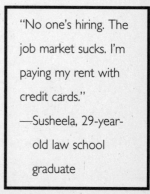

"No one's hiring. The job market sucks. I'm paying my rent with credit cards."

—Susheela, 29-year- old law school graduate

- *An increasing number of us think about getting involved, and value those who do.* Almost 45 percent of all college students surveyed

> "People in our gener-
> ation are becoming
> more aware. We're
> trying to be a little
> more concerned
> about worldly things."
> —Donnell, 26-year-
>   old medical student

by the *American Freshman* said that influencing social values was an essential or very important goal in life—an all-time high in the 25 years since the survey began. And one in three considered becoming a community leader a very important or essential goal—more than double the number who thought so when the question was first asked in 1972.

■ *More of us are starting to vote.* While national voting rates declined steadily from 1972 (the first year 18-year-olds had the right to vote) through 1988, younger Americans registered, and voted, in near-record numbers in 1992—the highest youth turnout in 20 years. For the youngest voters (ages 18 to 24), voting rates climbed 6.6 percent from 1988, the biggest increase of any age group.

Our involvement doesn't come close to matching the high levels of citizen action from other age groups, but it's a start. And in some cases, it's having a real impact. How much difference can an individual action make? Consider these examples.

■ *Wendy Kopp* wrote her senior thesis at Princeton on how an inexpensively trained force of college graduates could help revolutionize secondary school education in America. After graduating, Wendy put her idea into action. With a half-million-dollar start-up investment from Ross Perot, Wendy made an end run around the teachers' unions and established an independent certification process to train and place nonunionized teachers.

> "When asked whether each of us has an obligation to make a contribution to our community, over 70 percent of 16- to 29-year-olds said yes, the highest percentage of any generation."
> —Yankelovich Monitor, 1993

■ In 1992, frustrated by the unwillingness of their fellow students to get active about environmental concerns, *Brian Trelstad* and *Chris Fox* created Campus Green Vote, a nonpartisan campaign that registered more than 107,000 students in 25 states.

   They have now joined with the Center for Environmental Citizenship, working on the Campus Earth Summit and operating the Shadow Congress Information Network, an Internet mailing list that distributes over 20,000 action alerts on legislation to students in all 50 states.

■ *Michelle Nunn* started what has become one of the country's leading service programs called Hands on Atlanta. Today, her volunteer corps is comprised of more than 5000 people working on over 200 community projects.

■ In New Hampshire during the 1992 presidential election, University of New Hampshire students began a year-long struggle to overturn an old state law that effectively barred most students from registering to vote. Their actions enabled hundreds of students in New Hampshire to vote and helped lead to the enactment of a federal law to eliminate barriers to voter registration in all 50 states.

That battle became national as a coalition of youth, women's rights, handicapped, and minority groups fought to tear down barriers that tended to discourage certain groups—including younger voters—from getting registered. Although earlier efforts had failed, President Clinton held a Rose Garden ceremony in mid-1993 where the so-called Motor Voter Bill was signed into law, making voter registration anywhere in the U.S. as easy and automatic as a driver's license renewal.

■ *David Bernstein* and *Bob Luqfar* thought the traditional conservative view of the world was a little behind the times. So they joined forces over racial lines (David's black and Bob's white) to begin *Diversity and Division*, an innovative, forward-looking magazine to provide an alternative voice for younger conservatives.

■ *Gregory Watson* was 20 when he launched an effort to win passage of a 193-year-old, still unratified constitutional amendment that would prevent Congress from giving itself lame-duck pay raises. Frustrated about getting a C for a college paper on the subject, Gregory decided to show up his professor. He started a letter-writing drive that ended with 38 states ratifying the amendment—enough to add it to the Constitution.

- *Alan Khazei* teamed up with college classmate *Michael Brown* in an effort to help clean up the streets and the run-down neighborhoods of Boston. Their effort, called CityYear, put hundreds of young people to work on the streets of Boston—and became the model for the national service bill that Congress and President Clinton enacted in late 1993.

- Concerned about increasing threats to women—and spurred on by the Anita Hill testimony and right-wing assaults on abortion rights—Yale graduate *Rebecca Walker* joined with a handful of women friends in the spring of 1992 to found Third Wave, a new national network of young feminists. Their first project: Freedom Summer '92, a 20-city voter-registration drive that in just five weeks registered thousands of voters.

- In New York City, *Spinner Jones* educates adolescents about AIDS through street performance. At his performance space at 23 Avenue B—called the Collective Unconscious—Spinner works magic with a set of glowsticks attached to the ends of shoestrings. Like the Pied Piper, he captivates a young audience—and once he has their attention, he gives a talk about AIDS and HIV.

PLUGGING BACK IN

As each of the above stories shows, a single act can make a difference. But a handful of activists won't keep the train moving. Revolution by evolution requires all of us to make a little effort to bring a new politics of personal activism into our daily lives.

We're not talking about reliving the Revolutionary War or the antiwar protests of the 1960s. No fire hoses, tear gas, police dogs, or riots. Let's face it: Most of us aren't looking for unnecessary confrontation. A generation that reads *Details* and *Spin*, watches "Melrose Place," "Seinfeld," and "The Simpsons," and waits in line for the StairMaster after work is probably not going to be taking to the streets with guns or Molotov cocktails anytime soon. And why should we? Just because we're not prepared to die to eliminate the national debt or wipe out poverty doesn't mean we can't get involved in changing the country and protecting our future.

Moving from apathy to activism is not just about getting political in the traditional sense. It's not a choice between going to a protest and going to a party on Friday night. Activism in the 90s is about personal choices as well as group actions. You choose to use a 10-year light bulb or walk to work to reduce energy consumption. You wear a condom whenever you have sex as a sign of your commitment to preventing the spread of AIDS.

Saving energy rather than eliminating pollution. Stopping the spread of AIDS, rather than waiting for a government-funded cure—these are personal choices that also have political consequences.

In San Francisco, for example, one woman started a Safe Streets program that empowered community residents to shut down a local crack house and drive out the drug dealers. No police needed. No expensive lawsuits. Just a bit of knowledge about the law (provided for the residents by the Safe Streets center) and some persistence were enough to clean up one neighborhood.

It's a practical politics—just doing what needs to be done. It's about making a difference in the things that matter most in your life: having a good job, finishing school, raising a family, having safe streets to walk on, and living in a prosperous nation.

It's a politics that emphasizes open dialogue over smoke-filled back rooms, personal respon-

CYBERPOLITICS

As the first computer-literate generation in American history, our generation will engage in cyberpolitics. We've all heard of how the fax machine empowered the Chinese dissidents in the Tiananmen riots in 1989, breaking down communication walls built by China's dictators.

In America, with millions having access to computers, and massive networks traversing the country, technology is already far ahead of the fax. Within a decade, the Internet will become a powerful political tool that will allow a far freer flow of information between the public and the government.

No longer will Uncle Sam be able to put out a 2,000-page bill that slips in special perks and projects for members. Citizens will be able to fight back for pennies. How? Plug into the Internet. Get the bill through your own document scan. E-mail and umbrella grass-roots networks on the Internet will also enable activists to inform and coordinate the actions of millions of people.

sibility over party loyalty, and pragmatic solutions to solve common problems over ideological mantras to try to change values and create utopias.

Take AIDS, for example. Many Americans are dying of this terrible disease. They need legal, medical, and financial assistance—and they need physical care. The volunteers who provide these services are essential. That's one kind of activism. But hospice care, home-delivered meals, and bed-sitting clinics must be paired with political action.

In 1992, HIV infection became the number

one cause of death among men between the ages of 25 and 44, and
1993 was the first year in which
less than half of all new AIDS diag-
noses reported were among gay
men.

The ultimate solution to AIDS
is a vaccine. But that's a long way
off. As long as the government
restricts messages that tell people
how to have safe sex, limits support
to distribute condoms, and under-
funds education and prevention
programs, this deadly disease will
continue to spread.

> The number of
> teenagers with AIDS
> increased by 70 per-
> cent between 1988
> and 1990. By the year
> 2000, the number of
> AIDS orphans will
> exceed 80,000 and
> could be as high as
> 125,000.

AIDS isn't unique. Lasting, long-term solutions to most national problems—from health
care to welfare reform to fighting crime to wip-
ing out the massive national debt—all require a
new approach that combines service and
action, creating a new constituency committed
to ending the status quo.

AMERICA'S BALLOT-BOX GIANT

Citizen power always comes in numbers.

Just as it took tens of thousands of citizens
to end the war in Vietnam, win civil rights, get
a minimum wage, and secure the vote for

"Every day I try to do something to make our lives a little easier, or better. Like try to use just one cup. Or not throw out paper and recycle it."
—Mary, 26-year-old office assistant

women and minorities, it will take millions in our generation joining together to undo the failed policies of the past and create a sustainable future.

The more voices and faces in front of the politicans, the greater the odds of generating change. By 2000, our generation—those born between 1961 and 1982—will be the single largest voting bloc in the country, America's next ballot-box giant.

The under-35 vote could swing congres-sional elections in California, New York, and Utah, among other states. And a number of universities, including the University of Michigan, the University of Texas at Austin, and Ohio State, have student bodies large enough to elect or prevent the election of a member of Congress.

During the 1992 elections, groups like Rock the Vote, the League of Women Voters, the Rainbow Coalition, and Lead . . . or Leave registered hundreds of thousands of new voters—voters whose ballot-box action made a difference. The *Washington Post*, one of the nation's leading political papers, also credited the under-30 vote as one of the four key factors that helped elect President Clinton in 1992.

Younger voters also had a big impact in recent elections at the state level.

HOW OUR GENERATION WILL REDEFINE POLITICS

The Old	The New
left v. right	postpartisan
what I'm owed	what I can do
government secrecy	fewer information boundaries
Cold War	Nuclear Debt
mass rallies	local guerrilla actions
political parties matter	solutions matter
volunteering = a good cause	volunteering = political statement
voting booths	voting by Internet
special interests reign	search for a common agenda
everyone's entitled	handouts only for those in need
politicians-for-life	limited tenures
reliance on government	local and personal actions
leaflets	faxes and computer networks
politics = Washington	politics = life choices
evening news/*The New York Times*	CNN, Cable + Insta-News
small groups of activists	large number of once-a-monthers
ideological	pragmatic
polls	televised national referendums
politics out of the workplace	socially responsible businesses
dream big	clean up the mess
criminals' rights	victims' rights
electoral college	direct presidential elections
run up the debt	pay down the debt
industry over the environment	save the planet at all costs
Air Force One	video teleconferencing

- In Illinois, for example, Democrat Carol Moseley Braun became the first African-American woman elected to the Senate. Although Braun's battle with Republican Rich Williamson was bitterly fought, she was helped greatly by the 18- to 29-year-old vote—by far her best age group, according to exit polls which showed her winning 61 percent of this voting bloc.

- And in the 1993 Virginia governor's race, the college Republicans were credited as giving a major boost to the winning Republican candidate, George Allen. But even this increase in our generation's participation is not nearly enough to win the battle for our future. Of the roughly 45 million 18- to 29-year-olds who will be eligible to vote in the 1994 congressional elections, only 55 percent are currently registered—shutting nearly 20 million of us out of the ballot box.

Imagine how much more impact we would have if all of us, instead of just about half of us, registered to vote and then got actively involved in fighting for a new set of national priorities. That would affect our futures in very personal ways.

Take abortion as an example. Many women in our generation are pro-choice, not necessarily in favor of abortions but certainly determined to protect each woman's right to make

HOW WE VOTE

Smart politicians and campaign gurus are not resting on the laurels of their 1992 victories. Top players in both political parties recognize that younger voters do not hold traditional political loyalties, so a win one year doesn't guarantee a vote the next.

Nearly 30% of all 18- to 29-year-olds identify themselves as independents, and in 1992, independent candidate Ross Perot won a higher percentage of votes from the under-30 crowd than from any other age group.

After two presidential elections in which they could count on winning the youth vote, Republicans in particular are now uncertain about this powerful voting bloc and are unsure about winning it back. That means a battle plan to capture the youth vote will increasingly be an integral part of any successful campaign strategy.

that choice herself. But Congress and most state legislatures are dominated by older men, many of whom do not support that freedom to choose.

There are only seven women in the U.S. Senate—that's 7 *percent* of the most powerful legislative body in the country. Not very representative. What if every woman in our generation got active enough to ensure that more women got elected to state and national offices?

On economic issues the same is true. We see hundreds of dollars taken each month from our paychecks, money that is supposedly being put away for our retirement. We all know that's not the case, since the money goes directly from our pockets to a senior citizen's benefit check, leaving nothing for our future.

While many seniors deserve the support they get, an equally large number of well-off older Americans get benefits they don't need. And with a shrinking work force and a growing retiree population, the entire system is heading for collapse.

If each of us wrote Congress calling for Social Security reform, participated in a rally, or even talked to our grandparents about the need to fix the system (perhaps asking them to renounce their American Association of Retired Persons [AARP] membership or to speak to their friends about the necessity for change), we'd make Washington feel the heat and actually start revamping the Social Security system to be fair to all generations.

What happens on a local level, what starts with our individual efforts to fight for what we believe in, gets magnified on a national level. At that point, society—and politics—start to change.

The path from apathy back to activism isn't that hard to follow.

It starts with increased awareness, moves on to individual action, and ends up with a collective movement that involves millions of us in the battle to rescue our future.

Revolution by evolution. It will not happen overnight. Revolutions never do.

But if enough of us wake up to the crisis facing our generation and agree to become educated and active around the core issues that affect our individual lives and our collective well-being, by the time we enter the new millennium we will have created a new America.

Given the problems we have inherited, we can't get started too soon.

CHAPTER TWO

GENERATION DEBT

IMAGINE IT'S THE YEAR 2000.

A foreign power has just invaded America. Destroyers stand guard in San Francisco Bay, and off the coast of New York troops blast into the U.S. Treasury, stealing almost $6 trillion.

They darken our skies with toxic chemicals, infect hundreds of thousands of us with a deadly disease, plunge one-third of our children into poverty and homelessness, confiscate much of our income, and hollow out our cities and schools, turning them into war zones, like Bosnia or a set from the movie *Blade Runner*.

This is not the opening to a Steven Seagal or Bruce Willis movie. By the year 2000, this is what America could look like—a caricature of the strong, proud nation our ancestors founded.

If you're under 35, you'd better get yourself a shovel, because you're part of the cleanup crew. Every day that we continue mindlessly to empty our national coffers, we cripple our ability to award student loans, fight AIDS, clean up our environment, save our children, keep our seniors out of poverty, and create high-paying jobs.

NUCLEAR DEBT

Since the early 1950s, America has lived under the shadow of a mushroom cloud—the threat of nuclear annihilation by our once arch-enemy, the former Soviet Union.

Our fear of being wiped out by a Soviet nuclear missile attack was so intense that it fueled a trillion-dollar arms race and became the driving force behind four decades of American military, political, and fiscal decisions. The nuclear threat changed the course of our parents' lives.

Today, as the potential for an all-out nuclear war diminishes because of the breakup of the Soviet Union, our generation—and those to come—must struggle with a new and equally urgent crisis:

NUCLEAR DEBT: *a buildup of our national debt so massive that it is permanently* *undermining America's economic and social foundations.*

Today, the debt is $4.5 trillion, so large that if you paid a dollar for every seed on every Big Mac ever sold, you still wouldn't pay off the debt. You already owe $17,500 for your personal share—and because the debt is rising a half-billion dollars a day, that personal stake will top $21,700 by the year 2000.

Like a computer virus, the debt infects the U.S. economy, slowly eating away at our personal and national economic independence.

Just like you do with your personal credit card, America has to make interest payments on what the nation borrows. Uncle Sam's annual penalty for being so far in the hole is nearly $300 billion (up from only $19 billion in 1970). That's 20 percent of the entire federal budget, and more than the 1994 defense budget.

By early next century, interest payments could swallow half of our budget, leaving even less money for other critical social and economic needs.

Fact: Even if Washington makes a determined effort to stop borrowing more money, our generation will inherit, by the turn of the millennium, a $6 trillion debt— more than 20 times what it was when the first members of our generation were born in 1960.

That's right: There is nothing that can be done to prevent a $6 trillion debt load from being dumped on our future.

HOW WE GOT INTO THIS MESS

We haven't always been one nation under debt.

In 1960, the total national debt since 1776 was only $290 billion. We launched a revolution, fought two world wars, survived the Great Depression, and made America the most powerful country on the globe—all with a debt less than one-twentieth the size it is today.

In the past, we've always moved quickly to pay down our debt. In 1945, for example, we were borrowing $400 billion a year in constant dollars to finance the war; by 1948, we had already started to pay down the debt.

From World War II to 1981, the total gross federal debt as a percentage of our gross domestic product actually declined—dropping steadily from 120 percent in 1945 to just 33 percent. That commitment to lowering our debt burden was a key element of our postwar economic prosperity—and a sound strategy to ensure the economic future of the next generation.

But since the early 1980s we've been heading down the wrong path. In just over a decade, America ran up almost $3 trillion of new debt—more than three times the total accumulated debt from 1776 to 1980. If we'd racked

up all this debt to finance some dramatic effort
to rebuild our country—or to fight a war—it
might be excusable. But no great national crusade has fueled *this* debt binge.

HOW DID WE SPEND OURSELVES
$4.5 TRILLION INTO DEBT?

- *Military Spending.* Despite dramatic changes in the
  nature of military conflict and the diminishing threats
  facing the nation, the United States continued through
  the 1980s to spend over one-fourth of its national budget on military programs that did not best meet its
  defense needs and that had limited spillover benefits to
  the civilian economy.

- *Tax Breaks for the Rich.* The U.S. Treasury lost billions
  in the 1980s by giving tax breaks to corporations and
  the wealthy. The recipients were intended to pass on
  the benefits by increasing the number of high-wage
  jobs available, but the expected economic benefits ultimately were not generated.

- *Middle-Class Welfare.* Uncle Sam continued to give
  away hundreds of billions in federal benefits to the
  middle and upper classes. In the early 1990s, $120 bil-
  lion a year in federal benefits went to households making over $50,000.

We didn't go $4.5 trillion into debt by bor-
rowing to strengthen our economic and social

prosperity—to build a 21st-century infrastructure, lift every child out of poverty, make our streets safe, revolutionize our education system, or give U.S. companies incentives to compete with Asia and Europe. Just the opposite.

> From 1947 to 1973 it took 27 years for living standards to double. Now it will take 268.

What that means is that we ran up our massive debt while simultaneously ignoring vital national needs, such as:

- *Children.* Despite the proven economic benefit of investments in early-childhood health and welfare, we have an investment gap in the well-being of tomorrow's work force that the Children's Defense Fund estimates at almost $40 billion. As a result, one in five U.S. children lives in poverty—representing the poorest group in America.

- *Education.* Today, more than 7 million high school–aged kids are functionally illiterate. While many conservatives dismiss spending as a key to educational success, the U.S. ranks second from last among our 15 biggest industrial competitors regarding the percentage of national output invested in K–12 education. As a result, the American Association of School Administrators has declared one in eight secondary schools "substandard" places for learning.

- *Highways.* Since the 1950s, infrastructure investment has fallen by 1 percent of national output a year—or over $50 billion last year alone. As a result, our roads and bridges are in such disrepair that the Department of Transportation estimated that in one year motorists lost nearly three-quarters of a billion dollars in delays—wasting 3 billion gallons of gasoline. The cost of repairing our bridges and highways? Almost a half-trillion dollars.

WHY THE DEBT MATTERS

During one of the 1992 presidential debates, a young African-American woman asked candidates Clinton, Perot, and Bush how the national debt personally affected them.

All three candidates seemed baffled, answering as if she were asking them about the weak economy in general and treating the young woman as if she didn't really understand her own question. But many younger viewers knew what she meant, as America's national debt will regrettably be a point of reference for most of our lives.

The debt crisis is not just about a huge pile of money we owe.

It's also about the choices Washington

makes that affect our future—
choices that fund guns instead of
education, make Social Security
payments to the well-off instead of
lifting people out of poverty, give
subsidies to wealthy corporations
rather than assistance to small business entrepreneurs, pay for Star
Wars instead of AIDS research,
rack up billions in government
waste instead of lowering our
taxes.

> "We're like a new generation. We're not the ones who are going for the $100,000 salary out of business school like [graduates in] the '80s were. We're the ones who want a good job."
>
> —Marie, 26-year-old financial analyst

Our debt buildup has come to
symbolize the slow and painful
decay of America. It is an erosion
not just of our living standards but
of our values as well. We've turned
into a country willing to spend now, pay later,
a country famous abroad for our crime and our
debt. These are shameful measures of our
national stature.

Just as the Great Depression and World War
II became reference points for Americans raised
in the 1930s and 40s, the Cold War for those
raised in the 1950s, and civil rights and
Vietnam for those raised in the 1960s, today's
enormous national debt will define our opportunities and shape the choices open to our generation through the 1990s and beyond.

What kind of nation would treat its children's and its grandchildren's futures with such
meager concern—if not outright contempt?

"I think I should be making more than $6 an hour at my age, and with the monetary investment I've made in my education and the experiences I've had in other jobs. Honestly, I can't even really live on my own with the money I make."

—Joybeth, 24-year-old hotel employee

What does it say about our country that we cannot muster the discipline and conviction to live within our means?

By running up billions each week in new debt, our political leaders are not just pilfering our pockets, they are robbing us of our dreams and depriving us of the chance to do what every generation has done before: make America a better, more compassionate place to live.

Think for a moment about what we could have done, what we could have achieved of lasting and vital value with $3.5 trillion—the debt that we ran up from 1980 to 1994.

Sending a man to the moon cost us $25 billion. Building over 45,000 miles of our national highway system was a $129 billion investment. And securing democracy in World War II ran America $340 billion. Combined, these major achievements cost only half a trillion dollars.

What are the estimated price tags between 1995 and the new millennium to meeting today's big challenges?

- lifting most of America's children out of poverty = $230 billion

- universal health coverage = $900 billion

- linking every home and business by fiber optics = $150 billion

- providing a half-million new police officers = $100 billion

- tripling the research funding to find an AIDS cure = $39 billion

- boosting civilian technology research and development to match Japan's = $500 billion

- hiring a million new teachers = $250 billion

> "The way the United States is living right now is not going to take us into the next century. . . . If we decide to continue this way, we're going to eradicate a lot of things and we're going to wreak havoc on ourselves."
> —Eben, 25-year-old graphic designer

With the $3 trillion plus we ran up in debt, we could have achieved not one but *all* of these important goals. Instead, we have squandered our re-sources, making it painfully difficult for future generations to make new choices for a new millennium.

As a result, we are entering the 21st century deeply in debt—with little to show for our 20-year binge.

LOSING AMERICA'S ECONOMIC INDEPENDENCE

With each passing day, we are giving a bigger and bigger chunk of America to foreign governments. In 1970, foreigners held only $15 billion—about 5 percent—of our total public debt. Today, the U.S. owes foreigners more than half a trillion dollars—18 percent of our total public debt. It's a dangerous trap, like being indebted to a loan shark who can call in payments at any time.

Even the conservative *Wall Street Journal* warns that because of the rapid rise in overseas debt during the last decade, foreign investors "now hold the power to keep the U.S. economy growing, or plunge it into a recession."

AMERICA FACES FINANCIAL COLLAPSE

Optimists believe that we'll grow our way out of the debt, but history proves that debt-ridden economies don't grow; they collapse.

A huge debt left untended will one day trigger an economic collapse—fueling hyperinflation (imagine paying $50,000 for a Hyundai) and massive unemployment, putting things like home ownership, college, and a middle-class lifestyle out of the reach of millions, and unleashing an economic depression that will completely devastate the poor.

That's what happened to the Soviet Union and Brazil, where huge debt burdens eventually brought both countries to their knees.

As Brazil's debt skyrocketed in the 1970s

and 80s, the value of the Brazilian cruzeiro plummeted. Inflation, and prices, soared by more than 1800 percent. Imagine an apple costing $5 or a box of cereal costing $20. In Brazil, a cup of coffee that sold in 1980 for 15 cruzeiros would cost 22 *billion* cruzeiros today.

> During the 1980s, we added over $3 trillion in new debt. During the same time, the Fortune 500 lost 3.7 million jobs—nearly one in every four.

Brazil's debt became an economic leash, curtailing the government's ability to deal with any other national issue and destroying its credibility on the world financial stage. In the aftermath, millions of Brazilians lost their jobs, their homes, and their savings.

With each passing day, the threat to America grows greater. As respected U.S. senators Sam Nunn and Pete Domenici wrote in a wake-up call concerning the effects of the debt on our nation: "The Soviet Union sought for many decades to undermine the strength . . . and will of the U.S. What communism failed to wreak upon us, we may bring upon ourselves."

More than a decade and a half of reckless policy choices have pushed us to the verge of national bankruptcy. But time is now running out.

Early this decade, the U.S. government's own accountants prepared a major import warning of "fiscal catastrophe" if America did not deal with the debt in the 1990s. The report is stunning, since it was written by

HOW YOU FEEL THE DEBT

Fewer Jobs *The debt costs the U.S. economy millions of jobs.* Each day, the U.S. Treasury demands more and more capital to finance our debt addiction—taking away from the collective savings pool that businesses draw from to expand their companies. This practice raises interest rates and makes the cost of expanding or maintaining a business higher. The end result is fewer new jobs and more unemployment.

Higher Taxes *Rising interest costs drive up your tax bill.* Right now, interest payments suck up 40 cents of every federal income tax dollar—a figure equaling all the income taxes collected from every American living west of the Mississippi. When the debt tops $6 trillion the U.S. government will have to come up with $100 billion more in annual interest payments. That's equal to 32 percent of our current tax dollars.

Lower Living Standards *By the year 2000, the middle class will be out of reach for millions of younger Americans.* Predictions based on current trends indicate that in a best-case scenario, by the end of the century, many in the younger generations will be living at the lower margins of the middle class, or will already find it out of reach. Real wages have already begun to decline. In 1991, the average yearly worker income in the U.S. was almost $33,000. By the year 2020, that will have risen by just 5 percent, if the 1973-to-1991 income trend continues, to a little more than $35,000—far less than the rate at which the cost of living will increase.

Fewer Student Loans—More Expensive Homes *The debt raises the cost of education and home ownership.* A rising debt pushes up long-term interest rates, making the cost of home ownership, getting a student loan, or starting a business higher. Reducing the debt will lead to a significant drop in long-term interest rates. Just a 1 percent drop in long-term rates would lower the cost of owning a home by almost $1,000 and save the U.S. government $13 billion a year in interest payments.

government bureaucrats who aren't prone to sensationalism.

After extensive analysis, the nation's top fiscal analysts concluded that America has a small window—less than six years—to press Washington into action. After that, the debt will have grown so large that it will cripple our economy. Failure to deal with the debt crises in the short run, they warn, will crush our economic future.

Does such a warning deter Washington? Not at all.

Each year, the government continues to spend us several hundred billion dollars more into debt. Nineteen sixty-nine—the year of Woodstock and the *Apollo* landing—was the last time America had a balanced budget.

In the very *best*-case scenario, Uncle Sam will still pile on over half a billion dollars a *day* of new debt for most of the rest of this century. That means borrowing somewhere between $1 trillion and $1.5 trillion by the year 2000.

Why does it have to be this way? Washington claims that it's doing the best it can to bring down the debt. That's a lie.

A WARNING TO GENERATION DEBT

Just off the southern tip of Manhattan, a mile from the point where millions of immigrants

DIET FOR A NEW AMERICA

Imagine America as a 500-pound man. We've gorged ourselves on unhealthy debt for years now—at the same time denying the country the right foods it needs to grow strong. The result is that we're $4.5 trillion overweight—and in pretty bad shape.

Yet, every year Washington insists on gaining even more debt—and putting off the slim-down until tomorrow. Just another trillion dollars. Then I'll go on a crash diet. It's time to end the denial: Staying overweight will kill us.

There's only one 1990s diet that will get America back into shape: Cut U.S. government spending so that we balance the budget, and spend what's left over more wisely, directing money to programs that strengthen the country. Washington can begin by

■ ending funding for all unneeded and outdated programs, and eliminating all special-interest handouts—such as subsidies to the nuclear-power and timber-cutting industries;

■ reducing military spending to make our forces better suited to our 21st-century defense needs—and less costly;

■ making it a federal policy to give benefits only on the basis of need—which means no more medical and retirement benefits to the well-off; and

■ increasing spending on investments that generate jobs, educate our people, reduce crime, and bring economic growth and stability to millions of Americans—of all ages.

To trim down to size, how much weight would America have to lose? About $225 billion (roughly 15 percent of the budget), leaving us a federal budget of $1.2 trillion. That would be like a 350-pound person dropping 50 pounds—a lot for a person of average weight, but certainly not much for someone who would still weigh 300 pounds.

A PLAN THAT WORKS

Here's how our plan fits together. By the year 2000, we would eliminate $350 billion in current spending on outdated and unproductive programs. This would completely eliminate the budget deficit *and* put back another $100 billion into new programs and investments that would generate jobs, clean up the environment, reduce crime, and encourage economic growth.

These are not the only cuts or investments we can make. But if these choices—or similar ones—were made today, we would be paying down our debt and increasing our individual and national prosperity by the end of the century.

Spending Cuts $350 Billion

Defense	$69 Billion
Means-test all entitlements	$71 Billion
Package of domestic spending cuts	$25 Billion
Cut administrative costs for federal agencies	$16 Billion
Cut half a million civil service jobs	$46 Billion
Raise retirement age for Social Security	$16 Billion
Reduce farm subsidies	$4.5 Billion
Trim federal pension benefits	$4 Billion
One-year freeze on int'l discretionary spending	$5 Billion
Eliminate special-interest "user" subsidies	$7 Billion
Crack down on tax evasion and fraud	$8 Billion
Scale back the home mortgage interest deduction	$7.2 Billion
One-year pay freeze for federal employees	$2.7 Billion
Interest savings	$84 Billion

New Investments $100 Billion

Funding for all the proposals—including student loans, AIDS prevention, job creation, and ending homelessness—is outlined in Chapter Six.

ADDING IT ALL UP

TOTAL SPENDING REDUCTIONS	$350 BILLION
CUTS APPLIED TO BALANCE THE BUDGET	-$225 BILLION
CUTS APPLIED TO NEW INVESTMENTS	-$100 BILLION
YEAR 2000 BUDGET SURPLUS	$25 BILLION

"A lot of things are on our shoulders. A lot of people blame us for things. . . . [W]e're the first generation that's actually [been] put in the middle of it and had to deal with it."

—Ann, 24-year-old waitress

have first caught sight of the American dream, stands the Statue of Liberty—a symbol for all who have struggled to make America a better place for those to come.

A little over a mile away, in the vicinity of Times Square, is a large green clock flashing the numbers 4,561,679,000,000 (recorded on Tax Day, 1994)—the electronic digits spinning on and on. That clock monitors the rise of America's national debt, which escalates $12,500 every second, $750,000 every minute, $45 million every hour—over half a billion dollars a day.

Our national debt clock is a chilling contrast to the Statue of Liberty. It is a testament to the cowardice of so many of today's politicians, who seek political gain at the expense of their country. Theirs is a double failure: an inability to say no, to put an end to the unnecessary programs and unfair handouts that bust our budget; and a short-sightedness that blocks new investments that would improve our lives. Such new investments could help create good jobs, lower our taxes, enable more of us to afford college or training, clean up the crime and violence that rack our neighborhoods, and end the death threat of sex by finding a cure for AIDS.

But the failure is not just theirs; it is also our

responsibility as voters to make these changes happen. We need to tell politicians what we think is important—reelecting the ones who make tough decisions and booting out those who don't.

If we want to look forward to the next millennium with any economic security, then it's time to get a grip on our crisis; otherwise history will change our moniker from Generation X to Generation Debt, and we will go down as the ones who did not stop America's debt madness.

The only option that benefits future generations is to start paying down what we owe by early in the next century—*while the baby boomers are still in the work force and paying taxes*—and to shift billions of unneeded or wasteful spending into major new investments.

If we wait another decade to take dramatic action, not only will our economic and social problems be far more severe and thus more expensive to fix, but the boomers will be retiring and our generation will be left to pay the multitrillion-dollar cleanup bill ourselves.

As the U.S. government's own report concludes, "Tinkering around the edges only guarantees that we will have to deal with the problem again. To ensure an economic future for our children, these mistakes must not be repeated."

This is a simple but serious warning that none of us can afford to ignore.

CHAPTER THREE

AMERICA THE VIOLENT

THESE ARE the facts of Eddie's life.

He was born on a muggy summer night in 1979 in a dilapidated, dirty hospital in southeast Washington, D.C.—the sixth child in his family, a member of the sixth generation of black Americans born since the Civil War.

The doctor quickly discharged him to a public housing project and an apartment that he shared with roaches and rats. Eddie's home today? A different housing project, one on a broken-down lot less than three miles from two of the world's most powerful institutions: the United States Capitol and the White House.

They might as well be 1,000 miles away.

While Secret Service agents in three-piece suits patrol the president's mansion, armed gangs in baseball caps and baggy jeans control the territory around Eddie's home. Sirens, screams, and gunshots are the background noise to his difficult life.

Eddie's become accustomed to it. "You have to watch your back all the time. You can't go outside and play. You ain't got no peace," he says.

Gunfire, loud and long, scares him every night, making it hard to sleep. He's afraid that one day he will get shot. That's what happened to each of his three older brothers—and one of them was killed.

At age fourteen, Eddie is *officially* a seventh grader. He regularly attends school, but reads at the level of a second grader and does not understand division. It would be best if Eddie could start over again at a better school with smaller classes, but his teachers are afraid to hold him back any longer; they don't believe it will really make any difference.

Recently, Eddie was knifed through the chest in broad daylight and robbed of $5 in front of a public subway station as he was returning home from school. Doctors at Children's Hospital sealed up his punctured lung, but they can't surgically remove the fear that now walks with Eddie every day.

"The true deficit is not merely the trillions of dollars. It is a deficit of judgment . . . , of fairness, of concern for those deprived of opportunity or even the most rudimentary needs of existence."
—Richard Goodwin, adviser and speech writer to Presidents Kennedy and Johnson

COMING TO A NEIGHBORHOOD NEAR YOU

Like most of his friends, Eddie will be lucky to live to be 18. He'll be even luckier if he doesn't end up in prison. Nearly one in four African-American males between the ages of 20 and 29 is in prison, on parole, or on probation.

> "Violence in this country is destroying the lives of our children and endangering our very future. The next Martin Luther King . . . or Colin Powell . . . might not live to adulthood."
>
> —Arsenio Hall, testifying before Congress

For many of us, Eddie might as well live in Somalia. His life—and those of millions of other young Americans of all races living on the desperate edge of existence—is as remote as a picture in *Time* magazine of a country we couldn't even point out on a map.

That's a dangerous deception.

Today, in the most powerful country on earth, we have inner-city ghettos—and poor rural areas like Appalachia—that are little more than Third World islands amid a sea of middle-class prosperity.

These Third Worlders do not live a continent away, but in your city or your town—and they walk the same streets that you do. Most of them are trapped in hopeless, overwhelming poverty—a poverty so degrading and inhumane that it should incite our nation's outrage and move us to respond with urgency and compassion.

Eddie, and the millions of other children born into situations like his, deserves our concern and our help. Even if you do not care about him out of sympathy, however, you should care about him out of self-interest. Because one day, and in some way, all of us will pay for Eddie—either with a bullet in the brain or with the taxes from our paychecks.

When Eddie gets stuck, you'll be called on to pay the tab for his jail cell, unemployment benefits, food stamps, and hospital bills. And if Eddie goes to jail, it might be for a crime he committed against you, your friends, or your family.

> Every 100 hours there are 56 percent more young American men murdered on our inner-city streets than there were young American men killed in 100 hours of Operation Desert Storm.

Is this a callous and selfish way to view poverty? Or is it a realistic assessment of what will compel us to finally confront this deadly social disease?

Decades of government policy rooted in compassion, from the War on Poverty to a Thousand Points of Light to Empowerment Zones, have failed. If the powerful moral imperatives of crushing poverty do not compel us to action, our generation, and those to follow, can at least take a cold, hard look at the economic and social consequences of inaction.

TODAY'S POVERTY IS TOMORROW'S
TAX INCREASE

Today, in America, more than one out of every
five people under the age of 18 lives in poverty.
By 2010, according to a study conducted at
Tufts University in Boston, the number will rise
to more than one out of four.

In Detroit, of the almost 300,000 children
under the age of 18, almost 50 percent live in
poverty. Black infants in Chicago, Detroit, and
Philadelphia have a greater chance of dying
within their first year than do infants born in
Cuba, Bulgaria, or Kuwait.

Poverty rates among young adults exhibit a
similar trend. Between 1977 and 1992, the
number of 18- to 34-year-olds living in poverty
increased by 67 percent, and the real median
income of parents under the age of 30 fell by
more than 25 percent since 1973—after adjust-
ing for inflation.

Soaring poverty rates, AIDS, homelessness,
youth violence, Third World living conditions,
inadequate health insurance—who gets the bill
to clean up this mess? Uncle Sam. Where do
you think he gets the money from? Eddie?

NATIONAL ECONOMIC SUICIDE

As the hole in our social fabric rips wider, the costs of repair grow greater.

Each year, millions of young people—white, black, Hispanic, and Asian—grow up without the skills and education to lead productive lives. This permanent underclass will continue to suck up billions in welfare, social services, remedial education, public housing, prison costs, and skyrocketing emergency medical bills.

Perhaps today's older voters figure that it's not their problem, that they can save some precious tax dollars by ignoring and underinvesting in millions of impoverished youth. Our generation will have no such luck. We will be asked to foot the bill down the line—not only for today's poor but for their kids as well, the millions of children who are unlikely to ever outgrow poverty.

We are already paying enormous costs. In 1993, the average cost of treating a gunshot wound at an urban hospital was $25,000—enough to send a child to Harvard for one year. In 1994, 550,000 crack and other drug-afflicted babies will be born, the vast majority to poor mothers. The estimated cost of caring for these sick children until the age of one is $51 million a year. That's *today's* cost.

"When will we wake up to the fact that we are crippling our economic future by allowing the next generation of American workers, parents, and citizens to grow up in poverty?"

—Marian Wright Edelman, founder of the prestigious Children's Defense Fund

Remember, you're going to help pay not only for today's poor, but also for their children. The average welfare mother today is a 32-year-old white woman with two children—both of whom are likely to grow up in poverty. One in seven kids in America already lives on welfare, and an estimated 1.7 million to 2 million children are homeless. The lifetime aggregate costs of this public assistance bill are almost unimaginable.

The picture doesn't get better as America's children grow up.

According to a report by the Committee for Economic Development, high school drop-outs—more likely to have low-paying jobs and to be on welfare or unemployment—cost the nation more than $240 billion a year in lost earnings and forgone taxes, not to mention all the federal and state funding we have to pour into taking care of them.

That's with a national high school dropout rate among 16- to 24-year-olds of around 11 percent in 1992. Over 3.8 million 16- to 24-year-olds dropped out of high school from 1984 to 1992, and some were faced with unemployment rates as high as 40 percent.

In an agrarian society, or perhaps even in an age of low-tech industry, you could pull yourself out of poverty and into the middle class without a sound education. Today, in our high-tech world—where our competitors, like Japan, have safe, world-class schools, and the biggest employment growth is in high-skill jobs—those without a solid education are going to get stuck. But they won't be the only ones who suffer.

In a global economy where high productivity and rising incomes depend increasingly on a well-trained work force, an unskilled generation of workers means national economic suicide. We all lose if our work force isn't properly prepared to work.

Just as the crushing economic effects of the debt will at some point become irreversible, the collapse of our social infrastructure will one day be too costly to salvage. Already, many have slipped between the cracks—some with no hope of recovery, some of whom you may one day face down behind the barrel of a gun.

POVERTY = CRIME

Each morning and night, we tune in to the local news or read our local papers, only to learn of

AN APPLE A DAY . . .

The price of poverty—in taxes and in violence—is lower if we deal with it directly and immediately. Waiting until you get mugged by a gang or hit by a whopping congressional tax hike is foolish. Treating poverty—and its causes—up front will save us billions over the years.

- Fact: In 1992, the U.S. spent $24.9 billion to jail 1.3 million prisoners—a per-prisoner cost of $20,072. That same year we spent, on average, $4,000 per public-school student.

- Fact: Head Start, a federal program that provides critical support in education, health care, and nutrition for disadvantaged children, saves from $4.75 to $7 in future costs for each dollar spent today. Yet the program serves only 40 percent of eligible children.

- Fact: Every dollar spent on drug treatment saves $11.54 in social costs.

another drive-by shooting, to see another white sheet being pulled over a teenager's head. We read a story about 30,000 workers being laid off or an entire middle-management department being axed. We hear a report about our gridlocked government, a school closing, the ballooning federal deficit, and the tax hikes we're all going to have to pay.

The human tragedies are often more compelling, calling us to focus our national energies on issues that hit close to home: crime, AIDS, the lack of good jobs, failing schools, high home loans, and expensive college degrees.

Our failure of vision is that we don't connect these stories, but they are in fact inseparable. Our economic crisis has triggered a social erosion that has in turn unleashed the worst peacetime violence in U.S. history.

Generation Debt—welcome to America the Violent.

Our social decay of the last 30 years has produced a wave of urban and suburban violence unlike any experienced since the Wild West.

Today, crime in America touches everybody white and black, Asian and Hispanic, rich and poor, young and old, gay and straight. There is no longer a safe haven in this country, even for members of Congress and their families.

Images of the streets in America's inner cities could pass for news footage of any of the world's war-torn regions. Children dodge bullets on their way to school. Gangs, complete with arsenals of weapons and sophisticated intelligence networks, control the commerce of entire neighborhoods.

Prostitutes, drug dealers, and garbage clutter the street corners, and violent, obscene graffiti colors the walls, bus stops, and playgrounds—playgrounds where children die at recess, in schools with metal detectors, locked

> "Ninety-five percent of America's high school graduates would be unable to get into college in any other industrialized country."
>
> —Albert Shanker, director, American Federation of Teachers

"The light and excitement of the future/
Overshadowed by the gloom and panic of today/
No sun can be seen in the sky/
No sound of children at play."

—Ryan, 17-year-old high school student

doors, bars on the windows, and security alarms. And the schools lack books, adequate classroom space—and sometimes even running water.

As 16-year-old Stacy, a high school student living in southeast Washington, D.C., told us, hanging with dealers is cool: "They buy you things, they take you places. And after all, most of them will be dead soon anyway."

Stacy is right: There were over 18,300 murders in America's cities in 1992. In one week, during the summer of 1993, there were more than 25 murders committed in Washington, D.C.

The National League of Cities, a group that represents the nation's mayors, writes in its annual report, "City officials, by the widest margin since the survey's inception, report worsening conditions in the overall economy, unemployment and drug use" in our cities.

But it's not just the inner cities that are no longer safe. According to the FBI, suburban crime is on the rise. Violent crime has battered suburban communities across America during the last decade, with the number of rapes, robberies, murders, and aggravated assaults increasing by more than 40 percent.

4 IN 5: DANGEROUS ODDS

The number of murders committed each year in the U.S. is almost double the number it was 25 years ago. Sixty-five people are killed in America each day with handguns. Eight out of every 10 Americans can expect to be the victim of violent crime once in their lives.

Those who can afford to are trying to fight back. Security budgets for suburban shopping malls have tripled in the last five years, and sales of house alarms are up 80 percent from 1986 to 1991.

Likewise, the number of private security guards has more than doubled since 1970. Total private security employment now out-numbers federal, state, and local law enforcement personnel. Security guards now outnumber police as a percentage of the U.S. work force by more than two to one. And a growing number of suburban neighborhoods are literally walling themselves in—building gates and installing complex security systems to provide insulation from outsiders. An estimated 3 million to 4 million people live behind these walls in the U.S.—about the same number who are in prison.

Towns have built roadblocks and established checkpoints to act as moats around their communities in an attempt to reduce the traffic and criminal activity they felt would invade

According to the mayor of Los Angeles, a citizen of the City of Angels has a greater chance of dying from a bullet wound than from a traffic accident.

their borders from the inner city.

What's the point of earning a decent living, owning a nice home, sending your kids to a good college, being able to afford a new car—and then having to worry constantly about it all being taken away in an act of random violence?

But sealing off our lives and our families cannot possibly be the answer. It's hard to imagine constructing an America of middle-class fortresses without tearing apart the fabric of our country. That kind of class and race segregation could only be seen as a giant step backwards in the American Dream.

FIGHTING BACK

Should we get tough or should we fix the root causes of violence? Back and forth, liberals and conservatives have debated this question for decades. No one can pretend that there are easy answers. The appalling violence and poverty we face in the 1990s have been 30 years in the making—and they will not be easy to control, much less reverse.

But our generation does not have the luxury of holding such a high-minded debate, for every day dozens of us either become victims or perpetrators of crime and poverty.

While we were writing this book, a friend's roommate was murdered. Neither of us ever met Joel, but we will never forget his death. A guy in his 20s, he was held up at gunpoint and shot through the head while he was getting cash from an ATM.

Shot down over $20. It should have shocked us, but it didn't. Instead it became one more in a series of horrible stories everyone in our generation seems to have heard or been a part of.

Another senseless death. Another victim of random violence, undeserved and unavoidable.

We mourn the loss, take a few extra precautions—and go on with our lives. But that is not good enough, for what is happening to our friends, neighbors, and families in ghettos and middle-class suburbs and rural towns across America requires action, not talk.

A CAMPAIGN TO BATTLE CRIME

Back in the early 1960s, when we felt our national security was threatened by the Soviets' launching of the Sputnik satellite, President Kennedy initiated a historic and innovative effort to ensure that America was the first nation to land on the moon.

We did not look for excuses; we did not

MORE FOOLISH CHOICES

To salve the wounds of poverty inflicted on youth, you'd think we would be spending more to help solve the problem. In fact, we've pursued exactly the opposite policy. As more and more kids fall between the cracks, the safety nets to catch them are full of holes. Here are two examples:

■ Measured in constant 1990 dollars, the per-family average monthly AFDC payment (that's Aid to Families with Dependent Children—the government's primary social program to lift children out of poverty) has declined 45 percent from 1970 to 1993.

■ During the last 20 years, while the benefits of home mortgage deductions to the older and more affluent have gone up, the constant dollar value of a federal income tax exemption for a dependent child has declined, giving young parents—and especially those with more kids—less of a tax break for having a family.

compromise our people power or our pocketbooks; and a determined America succeeded. We must today harness that same sense of national purpose.

To halt the growing violence on our streets *and* to address the extensive poverty that underlies this violence, America will have to start walking two paths at the same time. We need

■ an unprecedented multibillion-dollar effort to crack down on violent crime; and

■ a massive new investment program that can
  help save the next generation of impoverished
  youth.

We need harsher criminal penalties.
Stringent new gun laws. Hundreds of thousands more police on our forces. We must treat
today's violence as our number one national
security threat. (Perhaps it is, given the fact that
more Americans are murdered in a year today
on our streets than U.S. soldiers were killed
annually at the height of the Vietnam War.)

At the same time, we must invest billions in
programs proven to give children the best
chance at escaping the shackles of poverty, and
we must reform welfare to limit the size of our
federal handouts. If these attempts do not
work, we must try other approaches—experi-
menting relentlessly until we get it right. There
can be no more turning our backs on America
the Violent.

In 1989, President George Bush told a trou-
bled nation that we had the will, but not the
wallet, necessary to tackle our most pressing
problems. He could not have been more wrong.

If we, and our elected leaders, are prepared
to make difficult decisions to reshape our
national priorities, we still have the time and
resources to fight back.

As we showed in chapter 2, we have the
money to battle crime and poverty if we want
to find it. Certainly it means giving up other

"Previous generations have left such a mess . . . [that] it's up to us to pick up the pieces. [We're] the quicker picker-uppers, almost like the paper towel brand . . . the Bounty Generation."

—Jason, 15-year-old high school student

things, cutting back on programs that are not as essential.

These will be tough choices, but they are choices we have to make now. Our generation must not yet admit defeat; we can't yet concede financial or spiritual bankruptcy. The stakes for us, and for Eddie, are too high.

CHAPTER FOUR

THE BABY BOOM BACKLASH

JANUARY 1, 2011.

Mark it down on your calendar. It will be the turning point, a watershed for America. Either we will have prepared ourselves for this moment, or we will have ignored the warning signs and moved toward a generational schism.

It's the year when the first of the baby boomers begin retiring, turning 65, all 56 million of them. From Woodstock to nursing homes. From LSD to CAT scans.

Advances in medical technology will help them to live healthier and longer, but will also place an unbearable strain on our economy and social welfare systems.

As they retire, as they begin their massive migration to second homes in Florida, condominiums in Vail, and modest retirement communities across America, a half-century of economic infrastructure could come tumbling down on the heads of the generation that follows.

If it collapses, the thunderclap will echo across the trading floors of the world's financial centers, through the sacred institutions of political power in America, and into the homes of millions of unsuspecting baby busters. The shock wave could blast people from their homes, rapidly plummet millions into poverty, and threaten the economic security and financial stability of our entire nation.

Those born after 1960 will face an ugly choice:

Surrender their future to the generation that preceded them—or fight for their lives.

A CLASH BETWEEN THE GENERATIONS

A quiet crisis is brewing today in America.

It gets little notice in the media and is rarely discussed around the dinner table, but it will radically change all of our lives. That crisis is the baby boomers' retirement early next century.

For as the baby boomers (Americans born in the post–World War II boom between 1946 and

1960) age, their economic interests will directly clash with those of our generation and the generation behind us—their kids and grandkids.

As they grow gray, boomers will step right into the shoes of today's seniors, demanding more and more attention be paid to the largest conglomeration of elders America has ever seen: over 50 million highly organized boomer seniors demanding extensive health care and retirement services from the government.

If elderly boomers want the same kinds of benefits as today's seniors (and most likely they will), that means higher and higher taxes on our generation and the generations that follow us.

And if today's politics are any indication, the boomers will have more than enough political power to win what they want—whatever the cost to those who come behind them.

With over 34 million members, the American Association of Retired Persons is already considered the most powerful lobby in the country—able to scare politicians of both parties into supporting virtually any policy it wants. The boomers' retirement will nearly double that power.

In addition, retired boomers will be better educated than today's seniors (the number of senior citizens with high school diplomas will double by 2020), which has historically meant a higher voting rate. They will be more affluent as well.

As a group of demographic experts warns in

Lifetrends, the baby boomers, in an effort to get age-related benefits from the government, could "come on like a political juggernaut in the twenty-first century, ramming their pet programs through . . . Congress."

The problem: Who will pay for them?

THE SOURCE OF A GENERATIONAL SCHISM

Strapped by a $6 trillion (or much larger) debt and an ever-widening social gap, Washington will not be able to continue borrowing to finance the boomer retirement without dramatically raising our taxes.

The U.S. Office of Management and Budget found that by the end of fiscal year 1991, the baby boomers had been promised $14 trillion more in federal benefits than they contributed in payroll taxes.

That's where the generational conflict will occur: Seniors expecting their benefit checks will be pitted against young families and struggling workers who will already be paying steep taxes and who won't want to pay more.

Everyone will be deserving—but only some

"I think [the baby boomers] care more about just making money and materialistic things and how much they can get."
—Denise,
    30-year-old benefits
    administrator

of us will be able to get a bigger slice of a rapidly shrinking pie. So Washington will have to
make a harsh choice:

- Sharply boost taxes for everyone under age
  65 (the Social Security Administration projects that the cost of Social Security and
  Medicare could rise to between 38 and 53
  percent of payroll in 2040);

- Slash spending on all other government programs to keep pumping money to seniors; or

- Cut benefits to baby boomers who've been
  paying into Social Security since their early
  20s and are counting on their U.S. government retirement check.

   In simplest terms, it comes down to this:
Our generation, and to a larger extent the
younger generations behind us, will be forced
to take another blow to our already declining
living standards or cut off a deserving but unaf-
fordable senior population. We will in effect
have to choose between providing for our parents or our kids.

HEADING TOWARD A CONFLICT

No one wants to face this kind of intergenerational tension. It runs completely against the

grain of family ties and social responsibility. As activists, neither of us has ever advocated starting a generational political war, and we have argued against those who do.

But unless America dramatically shifts our budget priorities over the next 10 to 15 years to create new policies that are fair to all generations, we will confront an unprecedented budget battle between the baby boomers and everyone born after 1960.

The signs pointing to such a battle are numerical, not rhetorical; they grow out of the economic and social trends that we have looked at in the previous chapters. They are based on reliable demographic and economic forecasts, not on radical projections.

Three main trends drive us toward a generational conflict:

- As the baby boomers reach age 65, America will have the largest senior (and retirement) population in its history;

- At the same time, the ratio of workers supporting those retirees will be shrinking, with record numbers of illiterate and poorly trained adults inflicting a drag on the economy;

- As the financial costs of caring for the elderly spiral out of control, we will be forced to cut or shut down senior programs like Social Security and Medicare (as well as many other government services that benefit Americans of all ages), or else raise taxes dramatically.

The genesis of potential generational conflict is that simple. As Wall Street banker Pete Peterson says, "When [our kids] understand the size of the bad check we are passing them, they could, amid ugly generational conflict, simply decide not to honor it at all."

If pushed to the edge economically, younger Americans, particularly people in their 20s and early 30s, would be the principal activists in this battle, taking to the streets and ballot boxes to demand immediate redress of their equity grievances. And the highly organized senior lobbies would hit back twice as hard.

Whether the youth of the 21st century will succeed in mobilizing enough political support to maintain generational equity is uncertain. But an economic battle between generations would be dangerously disruptive to America's social order and its economic stability.

At the state level, we've already seen how limited budget resources can force age groups to compete over spending cuts and tax increases.

In the early 1990s, taxpayers in Michigan and Wisconsin refused to pay higher property

> "I don't see our generation as being really content. I think they're searching for something. I see a lot of people rejecting what their parents have had or have done."
> —Elizabeth, 25-year-old graduate student

Social Security checks to people earning $100,000 a year are on average *twice* the size of the checks for those making less than $10,000.

taxes to fund local schools. The conflicts led to school closings and shocking pictures of 10-year-olds in picket lines calling to have the doors to class reopened.

Conflicts that lead to these school closings will only get more frequent, as America's financial resources become ever more limited thanks to the strains of a crushing national debt. The middle-class squeeze will see millions of us working longer hours for less pay, and we will all be paying the enormous cleanup costs that will result from short-sighted social policies.

Add the financial burden of having 20 million more retirees in 2020 than we have today, and a backlash against the baby boomers doesn't seem that hard to imagine.

Let's take a closer look at the three trends that are leading America toward intergenerational chaos.

Trend #1: Rising Senior Population

Around 2010, tens of millions of baby boomers will be stepping off the employment treadmill and into their retirement slippers. Once in retirement, they will make up the largest block of elderly that America has ever seen—roughly 20 percent of our nation's population by the year 2030.

To put that in perspective, in 1950, 8 percent of the population was made up of senior citizens. Today the number is 13 percent. California has a projected 69 percent increase in elderly population by 2010—and that's *before* the baby boom retirement.

The number of people over 85 (who are four times more likely than younger seniors to require expensive long-term care) is going to triple or quadruple by 2030. Never before will America have aged so rapidly, and with such startling implications for our national budget and economic priorities.

"The relevant question becomes: When and how are benefits . . . going to be scaled back?," asked one equity expert. "In a political crisis or gradually? Before or after we have sacrificed a generation?"

Trend #2: Fewer Workers

If the only issue were the skyrocketing number of seniors, perhaps we'd be able to survive their massive retirement. But the ratio of workers to retirees is shrinking rapidly—and that's where the trouble lies.

Between 2010 and 2025, the number of working-age Americans (people 15–65) will increase by only 4.5 percent—or 9 million— while the elderly population (people 65 and over) is expected to grow by 22 million, a 55

By the middle of the next century, there will be 1.2 million centenarians, up from 49,000 in 1994.

percent increase. In the bigger picture, over the next 50 years America's elderly population will grow by 135 percent while our working-age population will grow by only 35 percent.

In 1900, workers outnumbered the elderly by a margin of 15 to 1, so there were more than enough workers whether families were supporting seniors at home, or whether the government was providing a benefit check.

By 1980, however, the margin had shrunk to just under six workers for every retiree. By 2010 it will be down to five to one; and by 2030, there will be only three workers for every senior, hardly a ratio that is sustainable over the long run.

Trend #3: An Explosion in Federal Benefit Programs

In 1966, at the height of the Great Society, President Lyndon Johnson strong-armed Congress into passing a new tax on workers.

The tax was intended to finance a new health care program for the elderly called Medicare. Medicare was one of a series of government programs—like Social Security, farm aid, veterans' pensions—that were intended to provide a social safety net, lifting millions of Americans out of poverty.

These programs, called entitlements, now account for the fastest-growing portion of the federal budget. And unlike other items on the federal budget, entitlements aren't funded by annual government allocations. If you qualify, you get them. It's automatic.

Even under Reagan and Bush, two conservative presidents who attacked the so-called welfare state, benefits grew 54 percent (inflation adjusted) from 1981 to 1993.

Originally, federal entitlements made up a small and manageable portion of the budget: only 27 percent in 1960. But as benefits have become more generous over the last 30 years, we've seen an explosion in their growth; today they eat up almost 54 percent of all federal spending.

In 1960, we handed out nearly $25 billion in entitlements.

If the growth of benefits had been limited since 1960 to covering all new recipients *and* keeping pace with inflation, they would have been $176 billion in 1993. They were actually $807 billion—more than four times larger than necessary. One hundred seventy-six billion dollars versus $807 billion.

According to the Urban Institute, almost all retirees since 1940, whatever their income or family status, have received (or will receive) more than they paid into Social Security.

Why? Because politicans swayed by powerful lobbies keep handing out more benefits than we can afford—and sticking the tab on their Congressional Express charge card (to be paid off down the line by all of us and our kids, tomorrow's workers).

In 1965, for example, when Medicare began, the U.S. government predicted a total cost of less than $10 billion by 1990. They were wrong. Way wrong.

The program had actually cost us $128 billion by 1993—and the price is still rising. *For every dollar spent on Medicare, the U.S. goes 50 cents deeper into debt.*

Decades ago, as our economy was expanding briskly compared to those of the rest of the world, we could pay for such federal generosity. But today, with a debt crisis looming over us and a huge increase in the number of baby-boom retirees, we can no longer afford to sustain the explosive growth of entitlement programs.

Without fiscal restraint, before the middle of the next century workers will be paying over half their salaries just to cover benefits to seniors.

The Social Security and Medicare boards of trustees have already warned that the Medicare trust fund will go bankrupt within the decade, or earlier. At that point, the government will have to raise our taxes dramatically to cover the benefit demand—or stop paying benefits to retirees.

We can close our eyes to the problem, or we

ROBIN HOOD FOR THE RICH

Most of our federal entitlement programs—including those for seniors—have become a form of government support for the middle and upper classes. *Less than 12 percent of total federal benefits go to those at or near the poverty line.* Only about one of eight federal dollars of social spending serves to lift poor families above the poverty line.

In 1991, more than 40 percent of federal benefits went to households with incomes of over $30,000, and 20 percent of benefits went to households with incomes of over $50,000. The government wrote checks for $115 billion to people earning more than $50,000, and $30 billion to $100,000 earners.

Overall, the rich actually get more in federal benefits than the poor. In 1991, the government paid out an average of over $100 more in benefits to households with incomes over $100,000 than to those with incomes under $10,000. If you add tax deductions, those earning over $100,000 received almost 63 percent more in benefits.

can attempt to deal with it today, in a way that is fair to all generations and that protects those most in need of the government's helping hand. The costs of avoidance are frighteningly high for all of us.

THE COMING GENERATIONAL BACKLASH

If America does not begin to plan for demographic shifts ahead, a backlash against the

FIVE BIG SOCIAL SECURITY MYTHS & FACTS

MYTH: Social Security is doing fine.

FACT: The Social Security Administration predicts that
          Social Security could go bankrupt sometime
          between 2019 and 2036, unless we dramatically
          raise payroll taxes on the next generation.

MYTH: Seniors only get back what they pay in.

FACT: Wrong. Ida Mae Fuller of Ludlow, Vermont, the
          first recipient of Social Security, received
          $20,000 in benefits from a total initial invest-
          ment of only $22. But the economic miracle that
          benefited Ida Mae spells disaster for anyone
          born after 1960.
               Throughout the 1970s and 80s, most seniors
          got back two to five times what they paid in.
          Today, a retiree can expect to get back roughly
          double his contribution, while a 25-year-old will
          receive, at best, only half of what she is expect-
          ed to pay in during her working career.

MYTH: The Social Security tax is no greater burden for
          today's workers than it was for our grandpar-
          ents.

FACT: From 1937 to 1950, the Social Security tax
          (employer and employee combined) accounted
          for only 2 percent of a worker's paycheck.

Now it accounts for 15 percent—and is expected to rise over the next 25 years. This means that on $1,000 of income, your grandfather would have paid only $20, while you currently have to pay over $150—hardly fair to future generations.

MYTH: **Social Security is a trust fund into which you pay money that gets set aside, accumulating interest, until you retire.**

FACT: Today's retirees get their benefits directly from the paychecks of younger, often poorer, workers. Since the fund will most likely be totally broke by the time you need it, you shouldn't bank on it for your retirement.

MYTH: **Any change in the system will hurt poor seniors.**

FACT: In 1991, America paid out over $74 billion a year in Social Security and Medicare benefits to households with incomes of over $50,000—which means 500,000 millionaires get checks every month from your paycheck. We can fix the system to ensure its solvency for future generations and provide greater protection for the elderly poor.

By mandating private Individual Retirement Accounts, we could ensure that millions of Americans have adequate retirement plans—and still assist needy seniors (see pages 124–125).

elderly might be unavoidable, where reasonable but difficult demands for change from younger workers could mean moving retired boomers closer to the edges of poverty.

Flashpoints in a boomer-buster conflict might include

- rationing of health care to the elderly;

- shutting off the entitlement spigot, even to the poor;

- eliminating all tax breaks that benefit older Americans;

- shifting unprecedented amounts of federal funding into schools and training and away from all senior programs; and

- massive political pressure for a steep payroll-tax cut.

Before we're driven to this point, we need to take strict measures now. Health care rationing, for example, sounds draconian from today's vantage point, but it will be inevitable tomorrow without a dramatic restructuring of our economic priorities.

According to the Congressional Budget Office, health care costs will account for 18 percent of the U.S. economy by the year 2000, three times as much as in 1960.

With the very old as the fastest-growing segment of the country, experts estimate that a

HOW MUCH CAN WE AFFORD?

Between 1960 and 1990, the elderly population roughly doubled, yet federal programs serving the elderly nearly quintupled. By 1999, Medicare spending could increase by 67 percent while Social Security spending could rise 36 percent.

new 220-bed nursing home will have to open every day between 1987 and the year 2000 just to keep even with the demand—and this is long before the arrival of the baby boomers.

The cost of helping to defray the health care expenses of the growing retiree population will soon be enough to bankrupt many companies.

How will a company like the Bethlehem Steel Corporation—which has 21,000 working employees and 70,000 retirees—get by?

Instead of paying the higher taxes needed to finance the retirement health care of the baby boomers, younger workers would be forced to either form their own health care cooperatives (excluding seniors) or push the government to ration health care based on life expectancy.

Given the burst in the number of elderly, and the rising costs of their care, we must all face one tough question: Unless current trends are reversed, will we be able to take care of all our elderly—and still have the resources to defend America, invest in our children and our companies, and provide a reasonable living standard for coming generations?

Unless our economy grows at a record-setting pace, the answer must be *no*. Because of the confluence of the three trends we looked at in the first part of the chapter, the benefit package for America's seniors could eat up as much as 63 percent of the total federal budget by 2025.

Add in interest on the debt and national security, and that kind of spending doesn't leave much for anyone else.

ARMAGGEDON 2012

What happens if we don't change course soon? Let's go back to the future. It's January 2012.

Decades of mounting debt and unresolved economic crises have resulted in a time bomb, ready to go off.

The tension brought on by ever-growing tax hikes on the young, rising crime, and unresolved racial and generational differences burns like a slow fuse. Things are just like today— only the bomb is bigger and the fuse is shorter.

America has just elected its first woman president, an independent candidate who ran on a platform of tough choices, change, and restoring unity. But just days after she is elected the country explodes. A tax revolt coincides with the worst civil strife since the 1960s. The president calls an emergency joint session of Congress and goes before the American people to ask for order and change.

In her nationally televised speech, she will call on people to shoulder enormous burdens.

She will sharply raise taxes—including a 2.5 percent national sales tax and a 75 percent wealth tax on all income above $250,000.

She will cut federal benefits to millions—including student loans, poverty programs, and aid to farmers and seniors—and restrict all foreign aid, even to our Middle Eastern allies.

She will put a two-year freeze on all personal income tax deductions and eliminate federal aid to states, including K–12 education. She will shut down all federally funded low-income housing projects, leaving residents to fend for themselves or go homeless.

She will put federal troops in several large cities to restore order, placing a one-year ban on all private gun ownership.

And she will ask Congress to grant the president wartime powers—allowing her authority to censor, to jail without due process, to impose martial law. The country, she says, is on the verge of fiscal and civil collapse. These dramatic actions are necessary.

The president knows this is a dangerous precedent. She knows also that the country is about to rip apart. It is the day of reckoning. It has been coming for a long time. America must now face up.

THE ADDRESS

Good evening, America. Three months ago, I was elected the 44th President of the United States of America.

Tonight, as I speak to you, I have been in office only 28 days. The country has exploded with the worst civil strife since the 1960s—riots in our cities, secondary school closings, university demonstrations, sit-ins, and a rampant violent crime wave. Even the burning down of a nursing home. The very fabric of our society is ripping—turning black against white, young against old, and family against family.

For the first time in almost 300 years, our nation confronts a tax revolt. Millions of citizens have refused to pay Social Security taxes.

This is wrong. And yet it is not without basis. I watch my own children—children with every conceivable advantage in life—try to shoulder the burden of a 60 percent marginal tax rate.

I am not surprised that their far less affluent and privileged peers have decided that they can no longer afford to write the checks for my generation's retirement—for our second homes when they have no homes, for our advanced medical procedures when they cannot afford to give their own children vaccinations and basic health care.

This tax revolt threatens our country's eco-

nomic base and calls the bluff on over 40 years
of government mismanagement and indebted-
ness. Billions of unfunded liabilities are now
due. Millions of Social Security recipients are
demanding their benefit checks. Yet the trust
funds have already been spent—used irrespon-
sibly during the 1990s to offset the national
debt. And now the piggy bank is empty.

It is the greatest economic crisis since the
Great Depression. We are broke, save for what
we collect each month in taxes. And now, in
communities from Beverly Hills and Orange
County, California, to Social Hills, New Jersey,
millions in the middle class are threatening an
income tax revolt of their own. These are the
terrifying seeds of class and race warfare.

Less than half a century ago, America was
the world's leading economic power. Today, we
are the laughingstock of the industrialized
world. Our trade deficit ties our hands, costing
us high-paying manufacturing jobs and market
share in entire industries. We export jobs rather
than products.

A $15 trillion debt crushes down future gen-
erations. Interest on the debt, now our largest
single government expense, tops three-quarters
of a billion dollars annually. Foreigners now
hold 40 percent of the national debt—over $6
trillion.

America has the best health care system in
the world. Yet, despite numerous attempts to
reform the system, equity eludes us. We con-

tinue to offer million-dollar procedures to the few, while denying basic, affordable health care to the many. Hospitals in our inner cities have become little more than sanitized mortuaries for the wounded, and our infant mortality rate remains higher than those of Mexico, Bosnia, and Russia.

This is a crisis of our own making, and today we are paying the price.

It is time for new solutions. We must begin to heal the wounds that divide us along not only racial and gender lines but generational lines as well.

Had America responded sooner to the growing inequities that now divide one generation from another; had we found the resolve to live within our means sooner; had we realized the enormous social cost of allowing an entire generation to fall between the cracks; had we done any of this, my proposals might be unnecessary. But we did not. And we cannot go back to yesterday. We can only go forward toward tomorrow.

CHAPTER FIVE

THE TOP 10 THINGS *YOU* CAN DO TO RESCUE YOUR FUTURE

MINUTES BEFORE ONE of us joined Senator Phil Gramm (R-TX) on a live CNN news broadcast, the senior senator leaned over and said, "Up on Capitol Hill, we know your generation is in trouble. Do you know why we continue to borrow from your future, racking up huge debts? Because you don't get involved and you don't vote."

Like most politicians, the senator changed his story as soon as the cameras came on. He informed the national television audience that young activists like ourselves were well intentioned but misguided, raising the alarm where none was necessary. No one was borrowing from our future, he said. There's no need to worry. Politics as usual was serving the country and our generation just fine.

It was a harsh lesson in political doublespeak.

> "I'm right now actually on the verge of possibly going back and living with my parents, but I'd rather pitch a tent in someone's backyard."
>
> —Jonathan,
>
> 27-year-old law clerk/bartender

Senator Gramm, along with many of his congressional colleagues, knows that our generation is getting a bad deal under many current government policies. He knows that for decades Washington has taken out economic, social, and environmental loans against our future—and that one day we'll have to pay them back. But he's not going to say *that* on national television.

Why? Because that might mean policy changes that anger entrenched special-interest groups. Today, the groups with the most powerful voices in Washington are those that have informed and active members. Their members read up on the issues that matter to them, join advocacy organizations, and they consistently voice their opinions through letters to Congress and call-ins to radio talk shows.

Two years on the front lines of politics have showed us that this kind of individual and generational action has an impact. True, working at a homeless shelter, registering to vote, or holding a rally will not transform America overnight, but it's an important start.

ONE SATURDAY FOR AMERICA

Imagine, for example, if everyone in our generation took just one Saturday a year to do something that would better our nation? With over 80 million people in our generation, that would mean over a million and a half people each weekend would be out in force, helping repair America and fighting for a new agenda that would not only improve our lives but leave a better nation.

The following are examples of the kinds of actions that could take place in a single day:

- A million and a half people giving one day to volunteer to rebuild homes and clean up our streets.

- A million and a half people, on the same day, calling in to talk-radio programs across the country to demand that Congress ensure health-care reform doesn't bankrupt our generation.

- A million and a half letters to Congress asking for a new investment package that provides funding for training, education, and children.

- A million and half people protesting an end to the gridlock and reckless economic poli-

cies that have driven up the debt. You can bet
Washington would pay attention to that.

Obviously it will take more than one
Saturday a year to clean up our country, but we
can all start somewhere. Look at what happened in 1992, when 680,000 high school kids
made a commitment to reduce emissions of
CO_2—a greenhouse gas said to be a major contributor to global warming—by one ton per
person for the year.

It worked. By riding bikes instead of riding
in cars, recycling, and using energy conservation techniques, they reduced America's CO_2
output by nearly three-quarters of a million
tons.

If enough people made a similar commitment, we'd substantially reduce the dangerous
level of unabsorbed CO_2 in our atmosphere.
The same is true for rebuilding our cities, cleaning up our streets, and forcing Washington to
set new priorities for the nation. If enough of
us push together for any one thing, our collective actions will have a positive and lasting
impact.

Here are 10 simple things you can do to rescue your future—a countdown of the top 10
habits of good citizenship. Some are elementary, others may take more time and energy.
Start simple, but do something. They were all
designed to help you start plugging in to your
future and making Washington work for you.

THE TOP 10 THINGS *YOU* CAN DO

10) Learn about the Issues

You don't need to have a Ph.D. in macroeconomics to figure out that the national debt is a chain around your neck, or that there's something wrong when you have a college degree and are waiting tables.

But the first real step to changing anything is getting informed. And despite our worries, most of us look the other way when it comes to knowing the full story about the challenges facing our generation and how we can join the effort to meet them.

Only one in five people in our generation reads a daily newspaper. OK. You're reading this book, so you must care. But don't stop with the last page.

Real politics is about people of all ages talking and working together to solve common problems. You may not see it in the way most candidates and elected officials do business. But as a survey of college students' attitudes about politics showed, most thought that engaging in discussions with other citizens was a critical part of a better politics, and that only by listening to and understanding different perspectives would we arrive at the best solutions. Discussion, they said, was essential in making politics work.

> "Our generation really has to take the time to think about these incredibly difficult issues that face our world."
> —David, 23-year-old Spanish teacher

So where do you begin talking? It doesn't have to be on the pages of *The New York Times* or *Newsweek* or *USA Today*. Start almost anywhere. With friends and family. Do it in a bar. Do it at a club. Do it around the coffee stand at work. Politics doesn't begin in Washington; it begins around the family dinner table, at the local hangout, in the office conference room.

Ask yourself and everyone you know what you and they are doing about these problems. Only when people start facing the issues and talking about the problems will we get our nation—and our political leaders—focused on the solutions.

9) Volunteer

Volunteering is not only an important way to help people who are less fortunate, but it's also one of the best and most direct gateways to getting more involved in activism. And as numerous studies have found, our "apathetic" generation has some of the highest volunteer rates of any group in the country.

Almost half of all 18- to 24-year-olds volunteer at least one day a year, and about 25 percent of all college undergrads volunteer an average of five hours a week for a community service program. Through groups like Christmas in April, Habitat for Humanity, Do Something (started by "Melrose Place" actor Andrew Shue), and national servathons, many in our generation have discovered that getting involved in a hands-on way provides a far better understanding of community problems—and may ultimately lead to finding solutions.

> "I think we're a generation that's more willing to help the not-so-fortunate."
> —Lane,
>   24-year-old concierge

For example, if you volunteer at a homeless shelter once a month, you may eventually decide that you want to get involved with a nonprofit advocacy group that is working to end homelessness; you may even have fresh ideas because of your personal experiences.

Let's say you spend time working with disadvantaged inner-city children and see the positive benefits of public preschool care through Head Start. You may ask why the program serves only 40 percent of all eligible three- to four-year-olds, realize that Congress is shortchanging future generations with a poverty bill you'll have to pick up, and decide to help change the law.

There is certainly no shortage of volunteer organizations in the country and in your community—with young people heading up a large number of the most innovative and cutting-edge groups.

"There is a quiet phe-
nomenon taking place
on campuses across
the country: a surge in
volunteerism among
a generation of
Americans dismissed
for their self-interest,
apathy and nihilism."
—*Rolling Stone*,
   March 24, 1994

Some of these include Public Allies in Washington, City Year in Boston, the Boniface Project in Los Angeles, and Hands across Atlanta. If you're on a campus, the Campus Outreach Opportunity League also has the resources (and a yearly conference) to facilitate service.

Passed in 1993, the National Service Bill (modeled after President Kennedy's Peace Corps proposal) also makes available millions in federal funding to help bring more youth into volunteer programs.

If you're not sure where to turn, the easiest thing to do is to call, toll-free, (800) 879-5400 and find out about groups in your area. Other places to try include your local school system, a church or synagogue, the YMCA (or YWCA), or a volunteer clearinghouse. You can also check listings in your local papers under "Volunteers Wanted."

In the Action Kit at the back of the book, we've listed several hundred national, youth-led volunteer organizations, several volunteer clearinghouses, and information on how to get involved in the National Service Program.

Volunteering is a simple step, and a few hours spent a month to help a child learn to read, feed a homeless family, or visit with an elderly person in a nursing home can be deeply rewarding and eye-opening.

8) Take Positive Action

ADVERTISE YOUR OPINION ON A T-SHIRT

It doesn't get any easier.

Be a walking statement for something you believe in.

If enough people see the same message enough times, it eventually sinks in. That was a key factor in how the environmental movement got so many of us to begin recycling.

It's also how nearly every major product is marketed. T-shirt messages sell Nikes and Levi's; by repetition the message breaks through and convinces people to buy the item. T-shirts can also sell ideas to save our generation.

There's a grunge band out west that wears their Lead . . . or Leave T-shirts on stage and in promotional photos. At every rally we hold, we encourage people to wear our T-shirts. The people, the T-shirts, and the message show up all over the country on the front pages of newspapers and on the evening news.

Wearing your views is about the easiest way you can make a statement. Do it on your clothing. Pick a shirt/button/pin/hat/coat that makes

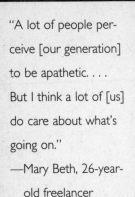

"A lot of people perceive [our generation] to be apathetic. . . . But I think a lot of [us] do care about what's going on."
—Mary Beth, 26-year-old freelancer

a positive statement about our generation—and wear it.

Other simple positive actions you can take:

- Send a condom to Congress with a note attached saying "Stop screwing my future."

- Participate in a bike/run/swim/danceathon for a good cause.

- Put up posters for your favorite activist group around your school.

- Instead of a throwaway gift, give a friend membership to a cause-related group for her birthday or the holidays.

- Put a new bumper sticker on your car every month—or any kind of a message sticker on the water cooler or coffeemaker at work or in the school lounge.

- Instead of money, give the homeless coupons for food—and give your friends these coupons to pass out as well.

- Pass out your congressperson's office number (and fax) at work or school and encourage people to call.

- Buy a CD whose proceeds are donated to a charity effort.

■ Sponsor a volunteer day at your school or workplace.

7) Join an Organization

Surveys of our generation show that most of us think organized interests get heard and have an impact on politics. As one student at the University of Minnesota said, the way to get your voice heard is by "joining interest groups that work on issues you strongly believe in. The only people who are getting heard right now are people who belong to these groups."

You may not like it, but that's the way politics works right now. And if we want to get our voices heard, we need to bring them to-gether into forums that can create the most noise on our behalf. The good news is that there are a number of organizations out there that are try-ing to put America back on track—and most of them, particularly ones run by young people, could use your support.

In the Action Kit at the back of the book, there's a listing of national and major regional organizations that are working on issues that matter to all generations. Pick one that is doing something you think is important, and join up today.

Joining a political organization is a great way to plug yourself into a larger network of people with the same interests and commit-

"The problem facing our generation is the government's over-whelming tendency to overinvest interest in one group versus another as opposed to focusing on a group that manifests the interest of the entire generation—or even the whole world."
—Stuart, 30-year-old architect

ments you have. It's also a great way to let Washington hear your voice.

A broader network leverages individual or small-group efforts, amplifies our voices, and becomes a vehicle for organizing and communicating. Like a collective laser, we can each use our energies and together burn our way through our common problems. It's already begun to happen.

Lead . . . or Leave has already established a network of more than 1 million young people across America, with community-based chapters in all 50 states and on over 200 college and high-school campuses, linked together through a national leadership advisory board and through the Internet.

The Campus Outreach Opportunity League (COOL) accomplishes something similar in the service arena, linking over 1,000 college campuses over the last 10 years in a community service action network. The bigger the national network our generation establishes, the more effective our efforts will be.

■ During the 1993 budget battle, Lead . . . or Leave joined forces with USPIRG, the Sierra Club, and a number of other environmental and citizen-action groups to form a coalition to pressure Congress to set new budget priorities (Green Solutions to Red Ink) that would curb spending in environmentally responsible ways.

Our actions sent a powerful message to Congress and helped ensure that several powerful industrial interests didn't succeed in completely eliminating environmentally sound budget cuts.

■ After President Clinton introduced the National Service Act, a coalition of youth groups formed to help lobby for its passage. A nationwide postcard campaign led by Rock the Vote helped swing the critical votes in Congress, making it possible for thousands of younger Americans to engage in community service in exchange for tuition grants.

If you believe in a cause, joining a group that is fighting for that cause is one of the best ways to make a statement of your support.

For example, if you're committed to winning greater economic and social empowerment for minorities, joining groups like the Rainbow Coalition (started by Jesse Jackson and now headed up by his son, Jesse Junior), the Black Student Leadership Network, MECha, Revolutionary Sisters of America, Freedom Summer, or Barrios Unidos, helps show our national leaders that this voice has a strong base of support.

You might consider making a small contribution to whatever group you join. It doesn't need to be more than $5 or $10, but it gives you a real investment in the organization and it helps cover the costs of keeping you informed and involved.

6) Do the Right Thing—Vote

As the Senator Gramm story at the beginning of this chapter makes clear, what wins votes is usually what counts. Politicians fear groups of citizens who go to the polls, and they listen a lot more to any constituency that can show high voter turnout.

> "The problem is people are not seeing a connection between the ballot box and the issues they care about."
> —Mary Beth Maxwell, organizing director for the United States Student Association

So it makes sense that there's only one way to change Senator Gramm's attitude—and you've got to do it alone and in the dark, behind the curtain at the polling booth. You vote.

The truth is, to have an long-term impact on how Washington deals with our future, far more in our generation need to vote.

If every single young person voted, it would shake up the country. We could elect candidates from our generation. We could reform our politics. We could pressure Washington to pass an agenda that deals with the debt, invests in our

HOW MUCH DOES ONE VOTE MATTER?

- In 1645, one vote gave Oliver Cromwell control of England.
- In 1649, one vote caused Charles I of England to be executed.
- In 1845, one vote brought Texas into the Union.
- In 1868, one vote saved President Johnson from impeachment.
- In 1876, one vote gave Rutherford B. Hayes the presidency.
- In 1923, one vote gave Adolf Hitler leadership of the Nazis.
- In 1941, one vote saved the draft, a few weeks before Pearl Harbor.
- In 1993, one vote saved President Clinton's budget package.

generation's future, and ensures jobs and economic prosperity for a growing number of younger Americans.

There are many reasons the majority of our generation doesn't vote. One of the most frequently given reasons is not being registered— and not knowing how to get registered. In fact, it hasn't always been easy to register. But in 1993, Congress passed the "Motor Voter" Act, making voter registration automatic with a driver's license renewal. You can find out more about how to register by calling your secretary of state, Lead . . . or Leave, or your local League of Women Voters. (See the Action Kit for phone numbers.)

As with safe sex, it doesn't hurt to be prepared—just in case.

5) Plug into an Electronic Network

Paul Revere rode a horse through the streets of
Boston to warn that the British were coming.
Our generation can ride the Internet.

Although originally the exclusive domain of
hackers, the Internet is now a forum for everything from support groups to stock market
analysis to cybersex. In less than a decade the
Internet has gone from use by a few thousand
people to being put into action by millions all
over the planet.

Today, the Internet is the world's largest
computer network, and for our mobile, tran-
sient, and computer-literate generation, it's the
highway that can carry our voices and ideas for
political change.

Electronic bulletin boards (or "news
groups") can monitor Washington, track elections, and inform people of rallies, events, and
happenings. And electronic mail allows you to
create networks of people with common interests and shared goals—and to be plugged into a
free worldwide resource of people and ideas.

Getting on the Net is not that hard. You
don't need to be a cyberpunk or a datacom
expert. In fact, you may already have access
through your job or your school. All you need
is a computer, a modem, and a guidebook (or a
friend who can telnet).

In the Action Kit we list some of the basic

PUMP UP THE VOLUME

Like Hard Harry in *Pump Up the Volume*, they broadcast clandestinely, beaming their messages over the AM and FM airwaves. These are today's radio pirates, determined to beat the system and get out their message. How can you join their ranks? Send for a radio pirate kit: Panaxis Productions, PO Box 130, Paradise, CA 95969, or get a copy of *The Complete Manual of Pirate Radio* by Zeke Teflon.

Internet resources available to you, the biggest networks, services, and forums, and a couple of the better Internet resource guides.

4) Voice Your Opinion

In 1993, when Congress was just beginning to think about taxing federal benefits to well-off senior citizens (or at least putting on the act of a convincing debate), we were on a national radio show debating with one of the leaders of the American Association of Retired Persons.

The senior lobbyist kept insisting that the middle-class elderly shouldn't have to pay taxes on all of their income—even though they were making as much as younger workers with higher living costs. We fought to make our case on the numbers and anecdotes, arguing that there was no good reason why a family of four making $32,000 a year should pay taxes but *not* a

> "I feel my voice mute in a world increasingly target-marketed for people with bladder-control problems and who need spray-on hair."
>
> —John, age 22

retired couple with no kids making the same amount of income.

Again and again, the lobbyist kept avoiding the substance of the argument, instead accusing us of ignoring the needs of the poor and wrongly suggesting that taxing Social Security benefits of middle-income seniors would push more elderly into poverty.

That's when Tammy called.

As outrageous as the lobbyist's charges were, nothing we could have said to him would have been as effective as Tammy's personal story.

Upbeat but frustrated, she told us that she was 30 years old, had just recently graduated from college, made under $9,000 a year, and paid $400 in taxes—a lot of money for someone in poverty.

To maintain her standard of "living," she had to hold down three part-time jobs. She joked that the only cure to her woes might be a husband, but wasn't even sure she had the time to find one, or that if she did marry him he'd make enough to keep them both afloat.

Tammy had always thought that a college degree would make her more employable. But it hadn't. Tammy had grown up believing that she would live at least as well as her parents. She knew now with certainty that that would never be the case.

"I don't want to live like royalty," Tammy softly told listeners. "I just want to get by and not have to eat powdered macaroni every night. My immigrant grandparents lived comfortably; why can't I? There are a lot of other young people out there like me who work hard and aren't looking for a free ride. What are we supposed to do?"

While Tammy's phone call didn't force Washington to change policy overnight, it certainly told a lot of listeners—far more effectively than any expert or activist could—that there was another side to the debate.

Voicing an opinion is a great way to start working for change. For one thing, it means you're no longer sitting silently, stewing over problems you think you cannot change. You're telling people about the problem. If enough of us spoke out, we would begin to see change.

There are a number of effective ways to publicly voice your opinion, from talk radio and TV call-in shows to writing a letter to *Newsweek* or your local paper or speaking out at a political forum like the Lollapalooza music festival or a Lead . . . or Leave teach-in. Each of these is a great way to enter the debate over your future and help shift public opinion. Take talk radio, for example.

During the early 1990s, when public-interest groups were angry about a late-night congressional pay raise, they convinced the talk show hosts to carry the message—and forced

GET ON LOCAL CABLE

Wayne and Garth aren't the only ones having a party on cable TV. In 1991, Lucy Symons, Hap Heubusch, and Miles Anderson launched "The Slumber Party," a cable talk show with a twist. While most shows have guests in their daytime clothes, the slumber party interviews guests in pajamas—and on a giant in-studio bed. "The Slumber Party" was a hit, winning the Home Town Video Award two years in a row. Call your local cable station to ask for a listing of talk shows. Find one that you like, call the producer, and try to get yourself on the air.

Congress to back down. Day after day, the hosts carried the message about Congress' chicanery and greed, ultimately compelling thousands to call the congressional switchboard and demand that the raise be blocked.

Although calling a talk show or writing a letter to your newspaper may begin as a way to get your voice heard and put your viewpoint on the record, if hundreds of people write to their local newspapers, radio stations, or TV stations, they can pressure the papers or the stations into addressing specific issues and giving them more print space or airtime.

If you go for a call-in show, be sure to have a pointed, coherent question (we find writing it out ahead of time makes it less nerve-racking). A clear, powerful question can significantly shift the debate and force the guests to wrestle directly with your challenge.

If you're writing a letter to the editor, read a few on the editorial page of your newspaper before trying your own. Refer in your letter to the article or issue you are responding to.

The Action Kit at the back of the book includes the top national and regional radio talk shows that you can call to get your voice heard, as well as a listing of the addresses for the letters-to-the-editor departments of top national newspapers and newsmagazines.

3) Call Congress

We won't even try to pretend that firing off that personal letter to your congressperson asking how he or she is going to address the problems that are threatening our future is going to make much of a difference. But it's still worth doing.

The best way to maximize your letter-writing effort is to send the same letter to four different people:

- the congressperson who represents you in the House of Representatives

- the two senators who represent your home state; and

- the president

In the Action Kit, we list the main addresses and phone numbers of Congress and the White

"I just don't get it.
Why can't the politi-
cians work together
and get something
done instead of this
bipartisan horseshit?
It's just bringing the
government to a
screeching halt."
—Kyle, 29-year-old
  actor

House—and tell you how you can find out what district you live in and who your member of Congress is.

Another strategy is to arrange a personal meeting with your member of Congress. Jon worked in Congress for three years and was surprised at the small number of people who requested meetings with their congresspersons—and even more surprised at the number of constituents who took no for an answer.

During the 1992 elections, one 34-year-old teacher couldn't get a meeting with House Republican Leader Bob Michel. So instead of waiting patiently, he went to a rally, approached the congressman, and in front of a lot of press people convinced him to take the Lead . . . or Leave pledge (a promise to cut the budget deficit in half by 1996 or not seek reelection).

So it's best to go with a group of friends. If you can, go as the official representative of a chapter of something. If you belong to the College Democrats or the Young Republicans or even the Junior League, try to get your membership to support the idea, and take a group from there.

LAUNCH A FAX/PHONE BLITZ

Tying up phone lines, with calls as well as faxes, is a 1990s high-tech way to catch the attention of politicians and to focus the spotlight on an important issue. During the 1992 election, 1,000 Yale students spent an entire day calling their two congressional candidates, asking them to take a pledge to cut the deficit—or quit.

So many phoned in that they tied up the candidates' lines, preventing almost all other incoming calls. The candidates, and their campaign managers, were a little upset. Their response: "You could have just called up and asked for a meeting." Yeah, right!

---

2) Participate in a Rally

It was October in Montgomery, Alabama, and the weeping willows were just starting to bloom when 15-year-old Todd Lewis decided to stand up and fight for his future.

All his life Todd had listened as politicians promised to fix the country for their kids and grandkids. So when George Wallace, Jr., the state treasurer, running for an open congressional seat in the 2nd District, started talking about the "next generation," Todd decided to call his bluff. What, Todd wondered, was Wallace going to do about the national debt and rising deficits that were crippling Todd's future?

The candidate was too busy to answer (after all, Todd doesn't vote, so why should a potential member of Congress waste his time?) so

"When we're born we get a birth certificate; and when we die a death certificate. Both are political acts. Thus, from womb to tomb we're political. The best politics are when all of the people are consciously involved for the common good."

—Jesse L. Jackson, Jr.
    executive director,
    National Rainbow
    Coalition

Todd decided on a more "in-your-face" approach. First Todd called a bunch of high-school buddies. Then he alerted the local TV station and his hometown paper.

Finally, Todd called his mom. She and other parents car-pooled Todd and his more than 40 friends to the rally point—City Plaza and the district headquarters of candidate Wallace.

The students chanted. They wore Lead . . . or Leave T-shirts. They held up signs and banners. And then they made their statement—dumping 4,000 pennies, one for each billion dollars of the national debt, on the candidate's floor.

The cameras caught it all—especially the angry Wallace aide who pointed his finger at Todd and said, "Very nice, son. Now clean up the mess you made." Todd, undaunted, said, "No, sir, that's exactly the point: You clean up the mess!"

Todd Lewis was just a kid. He was too young to vote and too young to drive, but he wasn't too young to fight for his future. Todd stood up for something he believed in. He demanded accountability from his elected officials—and he got heard. The 11 o'clock news in Montgomery is proof of that.

Todd fought back because he was angry and worried about his economic future. He realized that if he didn't get in the face of his local politician, Washington would continue to write laws that hurt his country—at the same time jeopardizing his own chances for a good job or a student loan for college.

Protests are a simple and direct way to send a message to our political leaders—from a small gathering of 100 outside a congressional office to 500,000 people marching on the mall in Washington, D.C.

When the British passed unfair laws to infringe on commerce in the colonies, America's first patriots dumped thousands of pounds of British tea into Boston harbor in protest. The famous Boston Tea Party triggered similar tea protests across the colonies. The movement—and the revolution—had begun.

Sometimes a citizen rally changes the course of history, but even if you don't rewrite the history books, an in-their-faces protest can break through the din of news stories, capture the attention of both younger and older voters, and make politicians jittery.

1) Advance an Agenda

As Virginia faced an enormous budget crunch in 1993, the state's politicians talked about tackling the crisis to help build an economic

---

BURN YOUR SOCIAL SECURITY CARD

You don't really need it since you'll never be collecting a dime, so how about burning it as a show of generational frustration? Imagine the message sent to Washington if 100,000 young people publicly burned their Social Security cards. Nothing ambiguous there: Our future is getting trashed and we're not going to keep sitting by.

---

base for their kids and grandkids—the sitting governor talked, and so did the two candidates running against him, and both of the seated U.S. senators up on Capitol Hill in Washington. So what did they do? The governor had proposed a 7 percent cut in higher education spending—yet the state had already cut funding to higher education by $413 million since 1989. Some solution. Balance the budget on the backs of students—and at the expense of a critical long-term investment such as education.

In Virginia, for the first time in years, students started to fight back. We spoke at and helped organize a rally at Virginia Tech that turned out almost 5,000 students—the largest student protest on the campus since the Vietnam War. Aided by our efforts, thousands of students across the state lobbied the state legislator and the governor to stop screwing young people and to start responding to the real needs and interests of the next generation.

The students got heard because they sent a clear message to Virginia's political leaders that, come November 1994, thousands of students would be going to the polls and supporting only those candidates truly committed to protecting their economic future.

Battles like the one fought at Virginia Tech are a great way to pump up the volume—coming together to magnify our voices and impact and exerting greater pressure on Washington.

The best way to win change in a democracy is to lay out a well-defined agenda, and then systematically advance it at the grass-roots level. That's what happened with abortion in the late 80s.

> "It's not really apathy that people [in our generation] have, but I think people are sort of overwhelmed with the state the world is in. And it's really hard to get a grip on what you should do."
> —Joseph, 27-year-old cartoonist

After waging a largely unsuccessful battle for many years to win reproductive choice rights for women, a number of prominent pro-choice and women's organizations, led by the National Organization for Women (NOW) and the National Abortion and Reproductive Rights Action League (NARAL), joined forces to mobilize a grass-roots effort to win passage of a federal law that would guarantee freedom of choice.

With millions of women (and men) protesting, writing letters, and tying their votes to candidates who were pro-choice, these activists were able to make abortion a touchstone campaign issue in elections across the country. And

> "The optimism, ideal-
> ism, and confidence
> traditionally associated
> with youth seem to
> have been supplanted
> by insecurity, cynicism,
> and apprehension in
> the current genera-
> tion. This survey
> reveals that youth
> (18–29) believe
> America is in deep
> trouble and requires
> significant changes to
> get back on track."
> —MTV/Rock
>   the Vote Poll.

in 1994, Congress passed an act helping protect women's access to health clinics.

Groups such as the NARAL, even groups that oppose gun control such as the NRA, get what they want because they have a clear agenda and mobilize an effective, and very vocal, citizen advocacy force.

An agenda for our generation.

No, there isn't a neat package we can all agree on. But there are a number of core issues and challenges that affect most of us, and that we can all rally around as starting points for change.

There also is something each of us could do today that would be a first step toward advancing the common interest of our generation:

Send a postcard to Washington.

If enough Americans demanded an end to the reckless policies of the last two decades, and if enough of us made clear that we would use our votes to back up this demand, Washington would stop finger-pointing and start problem-solving.

In this book you will find two postcards addressed to us at Lead . . . or Leave in

VOTE FOR YOUR FUTURE

(Name) _____

(Age) _____

(Address) _____

_____

Lead . . . or Leave
1606 20th Street
Washington, D. C. 20009

Please circle your top three issues on the other side of this postcard and mail to
Lead . . . or Leave. Postage is required. Postcards will then be delivered by
Lead . . . or Leave to the White House & Congress.

VOTE FOR YOUR FUTURE

(Name) _____

(Age) _____

(Address) _____

_____

Lead . . . or Leave
1606 20th Street
Washington, D. C. 20009

Please circle your top three issues on the other side of this postcard and mail to
Lead . . . or Leave. Postage is required. Postcards will then be delivered by
Lead . . . or Leave to the White House & Congress.

Dear President Clinton,

As a younger American, I care deeply about my future and my country, and I believe that the politicians in Washington do not listen to younger voters. I want you to know that I will register to vote, and I will turn out on election day in support of the national issues that matter to me. Below I have circled the top three issues on which I would like you to act immediately.

Jobs	Homelessness	Gay Rights
Crime	AIDS	Welfare Reform
Education	The National Debt	Other _____
The Environment	Social Security	
Health Care	Racism	

It's time you made new choices for our future.

_____
(signature/date)

Dear Congressional Leader,

As a younger American, I care deeply about my future and my country, and I believe that the politicians in Washington do not listen to younger voters. I want you to know that I will register to vote, and I will turn out on election day in support of the national issues that matter to me. Below I have circled the top three issues on which I would like you to act immediately.

Jobs	Homelessness	Gay Rights
Crime	AIDS	Welfare Reform
Education	The National Debt	Other _____
The Environment	Social Security	
Health Care	Racism	

It's time you made new choices for our future.

_____
(signature/date)

Washington. If you agree with their message, sign these postcards and send them back to us. Be sure to print your name and address.

We'll then send one to Congress and one to the president at the White House.

Here is our generational demand:

Dear National Leader,

As a younger American, I care deeply about my future and my country, and I believe that the politicians in Washington do not listen to younger voters.

I want you to know that I will register to vote, and I will turn out on election day in support of the national issues that matter to me. Below I have circled the top three issues on which I would like you to act immediately.

Jobs. AIDS. Crime. The National Debt. Education. Homelessness. Social Security. Gay Rights. The Environment. Welfare Reform. Health Care. Racism.

It's time you made new choices for our future.

CHAPTER SIX

13 CHALLENGES FOR THE 13TH GENERATION

AS WE'VE traveled to campuses and communities across the country and talked about the threats facing our generation, we're often asked, If there are so many problems, isn't it just too late to repair America?

Our answer: YES and NO.

Yes, if we wait for our parents and grandparents to do it for us.

No, if our generation takes the lead.

Older generations—in particular the baby boom generation—often appear stuck in some old ways of thinking. They were raised during the wealthiest period in American history— when America dominated the world economy; when personal incomes rose faster in one year of the 50s than they did in all 10 years of the 1980s combined; and when the country could afford to hand out government benefits with almost no regard to need.

Government worked for them, delivering on basic promises like a decent education, rising living standards, and personal security. As a result, they've had relatively little incentive to see Washington fundamentally change. Boomers and seniors who are accustomed to post–World War II prosperity have become trapped by the past and caught in a political time warp that judges new ideas by old standards.

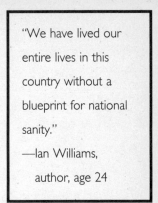

"We have lived our entire lives in this country without a blueprint for national sanity."
—Ian Williams, author, age 24

But unlike earlier generations, many in our generation see government—and politics—failing to deliver, placing far more burdens on us than benefits. Sure, we're grateful for our personal freedoms and our situation relative to much of the world's population, but we're justifiably angry about the problems that have been dumped on our doorstep.

Why try to fix today's problems with yesterday's solutions? Washington can work for our generation—and for the nation—but only if we force our political leaders to implement future-oriented solutions.

For starters, new solutions will require a new attitude, one that steps out of the framework of the last 40 years and looks ahead to the next few decades. Who better than our generation—a generation with the least to gain from the status quo—to push that kind of agenda?

"I think our govern-
ment is twenty years
behind the times. It
can't change fast
enough. All solutions
are rejected because
they're not perfect,
which sort of leaves
us in a permanent
state of stasis."
—Susan, 27-year-old
costume designer

With this in mind, we contacted two dozen of America's leading public-interest, community, advocacy, and youth groups. We asked the groups to help us design a bold set of generational "challenges"— specific, incremental steps that Washington could take that would help to heal our country and ensure a sustainable future.

We also asked for challenges that weren't limited by traditional politics. Don't tell us what's possible today; let us start fighting to define what is going to be possible tomorrow.

For example, passing out condoms to stop AIDS is likely to be perceived by most politicians as advocating promiscuity. For our generation it's as simple as saving lives.

Each challenge—from ensuring that federal programs meet an environmental "survival test" to controlling handgun violence to eliminating welfare for the well-off and reinventing Social Security so that it's solvent for the long term—fits the times and the needs of our generation. Each is also backed by one or more national organizations that leads in advocacy on the issue.

For example, the National Audubon Society, the National Wildlife Federation, and the Wilderness Society back our environmental

13 CHALLENGES FOR
THE 13TH GENERATION

CHALLENGE #1 CREATE GOOD JOBS

CHALLENGE #2 PROTECT THE PLANET

CHALLENGE #3 CONTROL CRIME

CHALLENGE #4 PREVENT AIDS

CHALLENGE #5 REINVENT SOCIAL SECURITY

CHALLENGE #6 DESIGN A POST–COLD WAR MILITARY

CHALLENGE #7 MAKE EDUCATION AFFORDABLE

CHALLENGE #8 GIVE EQUAL RIGHTS TO GAYS

CHALLENGE #9 HELP END HOMELESSNESS

CHALLENGE #10 GUARANTEE FREEDOM OF CHOICE

CHALLENGE #11 TRIM AMERICA'S BUDGET

CHALLENGE #12 WIN AFFORDABLE HEALTH CARE

CHALLENGE #13 REFORM OUR POLITICS

challenge; the Association of Big Ten Schools and the National Coalition for Student Empowerment back our education challenge; and the National Taxpayers' Union supports our proposal to hand out federal benefits more fairly.

Each of the organizations involved in designing these ideas will be working to win this change as part of their larger agenda. That means millions of people are fighting for each one of these challenges.

While there are many more good ideas than

the 13 we've outlined in this chapter, these offer a good starting point; they are each battles that will be fought over the next decade or so, not issues that will be resolved during one Congress, or even one presidency.

Consider these Cliffs Notes to a plan for national sanity—realistic solutions to some of the most urgent challenges confronting our generation, essentially the bare minimum that we must push for to protect our future.

CHALLENGE #1 CREATE GOOD JOBS

PROBLEM: Our generation faces the biggest job shortage since the Great Depression in the 1930s.

SOLUTION: As a first step to providing more permanent, full-time, high-paying jobs, we should increase our national investment in education, training, technology and infrastructure, and provide younger Americans more opportunities to develop critical work-force skills.

The good news: Since the beginning of 1993, America's recovery has generated over 2.5 million new jobs. The bad news: Many of these new jobs are part-time or temporary positions, mostly in the service industry—a step to building a lifetime career selling clothes at the mall.

Over half of all workers under 25 are paid hourly wages—which means no health benefits—and have earnings below the poverty line. Minimum wage has *26 percent* less purchasing power today than it did in 1970.

The largest private employer in the U.S. today is not General Motors but Manpower Inc.—a temporary employment agency.

"Honestly, I really thought that I would have a job job, a career job, when I graduated from college, but that's not a reality now for most people."
—Sandra, 25-year-old hotel employee

Manufacturing employment, where millions of our parents earned decent livings, is on the decline. According to the Bureau of Labor Statistics, the number of new college graduates will outpace the number of new jobs by half a million a year, every year, for the rest of the decade.

In the past, when the United States has faced this kind of "permanent" unemployment, we've done one of two things: tried to create new jobs by stimulating the economy through increased government spending, or cut spending and taxes in an attempt to boost investment and growth.

Today, we need to do a little of both, adopting policies that will restore strong growth in the private economy, jump-start job creation, and

This job-creation demand was designed with the help of the Progressive Policy Institute, a moderate Washington-based think tank with cutting-edge policy ideas. The PPI was instrumental in framing the economic platform that helped Bill Clinton get elected. For more ideas about how America can create better jobs and more economic growth, call:

Progressive Policy Institute   (202) 547-0001

begin to close our national "investment gap."

To undertake this effort, the United States should

- *Guarantee every young person the opportunity to enhance his or her skills through apprenticeship tracks in high schools, and provide college assistance for anyone willing to do national service.* The National Service Program, passed in 1993, is one step toward this goal.

- *Ensure access to retraining for jobless people and for displaced and low-wage workers.* This can be accomplished through "one-stop" assistance centers for retraining workers.

- *Increase investment in basic research, infrastructure, and worker training—three areas that will be underfunded without help from Uncle Sam.* Despite its importance to job creation, federal investment as a share of national output has declined by over 30 percent since 1976. Meanwhile, other countries such as Japan have saved and invested much larger shares of their national incomes. The result: U.S. job growth has slowed, while job growth in nations with high investment has increased.

■ *Remove subsidies and trade protections on most U.S. industries.* Just like you can't make new wine in old bottles, America will not create new jobs by protecting the old ones. A recent study by the Institute of International Economics showed that 15 of the 21 most heavily protected industries (in terms of quotas, tariffs, and other trade protections) in the United States suffered significant job *losses* from 1986 to 1990—and three others showed no significant gains in employment.

■ *Eliminate wasteful programs and tax breaks that insulate certain private industries from market competition.* This would free up tens of billions of dollars to invest in our future.

The harsh reality is that the job market is bleak—and will be for some time. But these five actions would be important steps toward solving our job crisis and creating longer-lasting, higher-wage employment for millions in our generation.

America should get busy and help put us to

work. It would be one of the best investments this country could make for the 1990s and beyond.

CHALLENGE #2 PROTECT THE PLANET

PROBLEM: The ecological systems on which we depend for survival are being destroyed and we're financing their destruction.

SOLUTION: Require federally funded programs to meet an environmental sustainability test, ensuring that tax dollars won't subsidize pollution and destruction of our natural resource base or encourage environmentally unsustainable development.

While some government policies discourage degradation of the environment, others actually pay people to keep doing it! The Clinton administration has made progress in protecting and restoring the environment. But overall, the United States pursues a pattern of development that is environmentally unsustainable.

Consider these facts:

- The United States comprises only 5 percent of the world's population but consumes over 30 percent of its nonrenewable resources.

- According to the Union of Concerned Scientists, 92.5 percent of U.S. energy consumption comes from nonrenewable resources.

- The average U.S. citizen produces 1,584 pounds of garbage per year—approximately 52 tons over a lifetime. That compares to 902 pounds for the average citizen of Japan and 660 pounds for the average European citizen.

- Less than 50 percent of our original wetlands, 5 to 7 percent of our Northwest ancient forests, and 4 percent of our original wilderness lands still remain.

We can't keep dumping toxic wastes, contaminating our groundwater, using up our nonrenewable resources, destroying the ozone layer, and exterminating other species faster than we can name them. Eventually, someone's going to have to pay for today's reckless environmental destruction.

Some interests want us to think that environmental protection costs too much. They want us to believe that a degraded environment won't cost us anything. But the fact is, our tax dollars are used to clean up their toxic messes and subsidize their destructive practices.

"It's not really about spotted owls versus lumberjacks. Toxic waste. Global warming. Acid rain. We're consuming ourselves out of existence. Either we start making new choices or our kids will have to live in plastic bubbles."
—Lisa, 27-year-old
    environmental
    activist

Worse, we're leaving an environmental debt! Present and future generations will pay not only with their dollars but with their health, standard of living, and quality of life. Each one of us needs to examine our personal choices and how they affect the environment over the long term. At the same time, we can't allow our government to encourage environmental degradation with our tax dollars.

No more subsidies for companies who cut timber from federal lands—they cost us over $500 million a year. No more royalty-free mining on public lands—we lose billions on this one. No more military bombing runs over national wildlife refuges. No more incentives for people to build shopping malls in fragile coastal areas. No more pretending that environmental protection costs more than environmental destruction.

Every federal program should meet a set of environmental sustainability standards that determine whether it complies with national pollution standards, promotes sound natural resource management and conservation, encourages balanced population distribution, contributes to energy efficiency, and increases reliance on renewable resources.

This proposal is endorsed by the National Audubon Society, the National Wildlife Federation, and the Wilderness Society, three of the oldest and largest environmental groups in America. To find out more about how you can win the fight for an environmentally sustainable future, contact:

National Audubon Society (202) 547-9009
National Wildlife Federation (202) 797-6800
The Wilderness Society (202) 833-2300

CHALLENGE #3 CONTROL CRIME

PROBLEM: Gun violence is slowly destroying the American dream and is driving a crime spree that costs the country over $650 billion a year in police, private security, and lost productivity.

SOLUTION: As part of a comprehensive control strategy, require an owner's license and registration of gun transfers.

What gives? Americans are shooting each other by the thousands every year—and virtually every poll shows strong public support for regulating handguns and semiautomatics—yet it took Washington almost seven years to pass

> "I've been held up twice at gunpoint. My sister was raped and murdered and two of my band members were severely assaulted. It's a huge part of my life. It's easy to bitch about it, but at this point, I'd rather take part in the solution."
>
> —Fire, 28-year-old musician

the Brady Bill's seven-day waiting period for the purchase of guns.

As groups like the Violence Policy Center and Handgun Control Inc. point out, there is "a gun crisis in the United States." Since 1960, over 500,000 Americans were killed by firearms, and today, "among all consumer products, only cars outpace guns as a cause of fatal injury, and guns will likely pass them by 2003." And the Centers for Disease Control estimated the 1985 cost (latest available) of firearms violence at $14.4 billion, which places a heavy economic toll on the nation.

Contradicting common perception, most murders are not committed by strangers but by people the victims knew. According to the Violence Prevention Center, "the majority of firearms homicide stems from arguments that turn deadly because of ready access to a gun."

Nor is most murder interracial. In 1992, for example, 94 percent of black murder victims were killed by blacks and 83 percent of white victims were slain by white offenders. Guns are killing every race in America—and every year handguns are used in over 800,000 violent crimes.

If we're going to get at the root of the problem, we'll have to learn to treat a gun just like

Handgun Control Inc., the author of the Brady Bill and one of the nation's top advocates for gun sanity, helped us frame this issue and has designed a plan to register and license all handguns. To find out more about the plan, and how we can win comprehensive gun regulation, contact:

Handgun Control Inc.   (202) 898-0792

the other deadly weapon consumers regularly purchase: a car. That means gun ownership and sales should be subject to restrictions similar to those placed on the sales and ownership of cars.

Such restrictions must include two key requirements: (1) a person must obtain a handgun license to possess a handgun or ammunition; and (2) anyone selling or giving away a gun must register the transfer with a state agency (just as you do when swapping the title for a car). Failure to register the transfer would make you eligible for state prosecution that could result in a tough prison term. Legislating that kind of direct personal responsibility would make gun owners far more cautious about who has access to their guns (and who they might sell them to).

Our generation must not be held hostage to the gun lobbies; we can break the logjam, protecting the rights of gun owners and dramatically cutting back on gun violence. It's a battle we can help win.

CHALLENGE #4 PREVENT AIDS

PROBLEM: AIDS

SOLUTION: Get the word out! We need
              more aggressive and effective
              AIDS prevention programs for
              young people.

Every six minutes, another person dies of
AIDS in the United States. Today more
Americans have died of AIDS than in the Gulf,
Vietnam, and Korean wars combined. Already
more than 1 million Americans are infected
with HIV, the virus that causes AIDS—and that
number grows by the tens of thousands each
year, with the largest proportionate increase in
AIDS cases among heterosexuals.

People from 20- to 35-years-old represent
almost half of the total cases of AIDS in the
U.S., and in 64 major U.S. cities AIDS is the
number one killer of young Americans.
Nationally it's the leading killer of men between
the ages of 25 and 44 and the number four
killer of women in that age group.

It is estimated that by the year 2000, 45 million to 110 million men, women, and children
on the planet will be infected with HIV. That
would be like everyone in all the states west of
the Mississippi—except California—having
HIV. The high estimate is equal to almost

half of the U.S. population. Imagine if half the people you knew were doomed to die from AIDS.

HIV infection may not yet be curable, but it is preventable. The U.S. government has failed to mount aggressive and explicit HIV prevention campaigns that talk frankly about how you can get

> "People no longer live in fear of nuclear war. Now they live in fear of AIDS."
> —Chuck, 23-year-old student / waiter

HIV and how you can avoid it. After more than a decade of stringent content restrictions on federally funded prevention programs, the federal government has at last produced public-service announcements for television promoting the use of latex condoms as an effective way to prevent the spread of HIV. It's a first step, but not enough.

The federal government needs to fund more and better AIDS prevention and education programs. At the same time, we need to encourage local schools and communities to provide young people with information about condoms and make them easily available for sexually active young people. Moralizing won't stop the spread of AIDS—condoms and other education and prevention programs will.

The following are things the government can do to meet this challenge:

■ *Increase federal funding for AIDS prevention*
　To help win the fight against AIDS, the

According to the *Yankelovich Monitor,* 82 percent of 16- to 29-year-olds support AIDS education in schools and public-service ads about AIDS—the highest percentage of any generation.

federal government should increase funding for AIDS prevention programs by at least 35 percent, up from the current level of $543 million to $733 million, enabling a significant increase in public-service announcements and street outreach and condom availability programs.

- *Make condoms freely available to sexually active young people*

Using a condom is an act of personal protection, the ultimate sign of taking responsibility for your life. Whatever your beliefs about sexual activity, the reality is that, outside of abstinence, only condoms help stop the spread of AIDS. Encourage your local community leaders to make condoms available to youth and young adults through schools, health centers, recreation facilities, and other places accessible to youth.

The Washington-based **AIDS Action Council,** a top advocate in the battle against AIDS, helped us design this proposal and is a leader in the effort to win increased funding for AIDS prevention. To find out more about what you can do to help prevent the spread of AIDS in your community, call your local AIDS service organization or call **(800) 342-AIDS** to find the local AIDS group nearest you.

Other things you can do:

■ *Increase the education of AIDS prevention in schools*

Encourage your local school board to adopt a comprehensive program for prevention of HIV that encourages young people to delay sexual intercourse and teaches them about the use of condoms for when they decide to have sexual intercourse.

■ *Clean needles reduce the spread of AIDS*

Organize activists to start a needle exchange program. HIV is often transmitted when IV drug users share needles. While controversial, needle exchange projects make clean needles available to IV drug users and reduce the spread of HIV.

■ *More AIDS prevention messages on TV*

Pressure television networks and local stations to air public-service announcements that talk frankly about AIDS prevention and condoms.

> "The devastating thing about [AIDS] is that it isn't very selective. The demographics of who's infected are changing and it's starting to affect the mainstay of the population: the adolescents, heterosexuals (especially women), and increasingly teenagers."
>
> —Rick, 29-year-old actor

CHALLENGE #5 REINVENT SOCIAL SECURITY

PROBLEM: As the baby boomers retire, the
          U.S. will no longer be able to
          afford to pay out Social Security
          benefits without drastically rais-
          ing taxes on younger workers.

SOLUTION: Reinvent Social Security now in a
          way that is fair to all genera-
          tions—and protects today's at-
          risk seniors.

Currently, we're bringing in enough money
to finance Social Security, but the U.S. Social
Security Administration projects that Social
Security could be broke by 2020. Even their
most optimistic scenario projects insolvency no
later than 2029.

Contrary to common perception, Social
Security is not a trust fund, into which your
contributions are put aside—and saved—until
you retire, like a big national piggy bank. Instead, today's retirees get their benefits directly
from the paychecks of working Americans.

And it's often not a fair trade. A kid flipping
burgers at five bucks an hour still pays the
Social Security benefits of a retired couple living
in Florida with a cash income of $50,000 a year
and a paid-off mortgage.

Today's Social Security system is unfair and

heading for collapse. While it worked for older generations, it is certain to penalize most in our generation (we'll be lucky to get any return on what we pay in).

So how do we fix the problem? We've got to adopt a new standard for federal assistance: Take only what you need, not what you want or think you deserve. Although many government programs give you benefits *only* if you need them—including food stamps, child nutrition, and student loans—this is not so for programs targeted at the elderly.

"The government is the same as it's ever been. They've never been on our side, even though they take our money. . . . Some of them really want to help us, but they don't know how."
—Norberto, 31-year-old actor

No matter how rich you are, you are entitled to Social Security and Medicare. That means Johnny Carson and Leona Helmsley are both entitled to a federal check. Talk about welfare for the well-off.

To fix this, we need an "affluence" test for all recipients of federal benefits, where everyone earning more than $40,000 a year—working or retired—would get fewer benefits. (*Not one dime in benefits would be taken away if you earn less than the median income of $40,000*).

A family earning $45,000 would lose only about $260 in benefits; one earning over $75,000 would lose $4,500; and one earning over $200,000 would still get 25 percent of its benefits. That's fair.

This generationally fair benefits means-test has been endorsed by the National Taxpayers' Union, Citizens for a Sound Economy, and the American Association of Boomers.

NTU has 250,000 members and fights for taxpayer savings, holding Congress's feet to the fire on many spending issues.

CSE is a 250,000-member grass-roots lobbying organization promoting a free-market economy and the lifting of government taxes and regulation.

The formation of a private Social Security system is backed by the American Association of Boomers, the leading advocacy group for boomers, although their membership benefits are available to anyone.

To reach these groups, call:

National Taxpayers' Union   (202) 543-1300
Citizens for a Sound Economy   (800) 925-7921
American Association of Boomers   (800) BOOMERS

An affluence test on the well-off, however, is only a stopgap measure for Social Security, not a long-term solution. Ultimately, we will have to shift to a federally backed private pension system, which would let people opt out of Social Security and save privately for their retirement.

Here's how it would work.

First, we would have to make IRAs (individual retirement accounts) mandatory, and eliminate (or substantially raise) the deductible limits. If you haven't done this already, look at your paycheck. Let's say you make $25,000 a year. Combining what you and your employer pay to Social Security, you could be saving almost $4,000 a year in a personal pension fund or savings account.

If you put away just half that amount—$2,000 a year—for more than 40 years at a modest 5 percent interest rate, you would save over a quarter million for retirement. And that's money you'd be certain to get back.

Saving could not be optional; the government would have to mandate that a set portion of your paycheck was set aside and placed in a private retirement account. As for those in need, the answer is to remove the welfare part of Social Security from the rest of the retirement system. Welfare for the elderly would come from general revenues—like all other welfare programs—and IRAs would cover all nonwelfare retirement. For just $15 billion a year, we could lift most of today's seniors out of poverty.

A private pension system based on mandatory IRAs—combined with an increase in benefit checks to poor seniors—would ensure the long-term solvency of America's retirement system, increasing economic security, preventing collapse of the current Social Security system, and protecting a greater percentage of today's elderly poor.

CHALLENGE #6 DESIGN A POST–COLD WAR MILITARY

PROBLEM: In the post–Cold War world, the U.S. military is no longer structured to meet real national security challenges and is wasting scarce resources.

SOLUTION: Reshape our military to meet emerging global threats, ensure a strong national defense, *and* save taxpayers billions.

The United States spends more than $280 billion annually on the military. That's more than is spent by the 10 next-highest-ranking military powers *combined*—most of whom are our allies. Even with currently proposed reductions, the United States will spend around $230 billion a year by 2000, almost three times the combined amount to be spent by our potential *adversaries*—including Russia, Iraq, China, Iran, North Korea, and Libya.

We do not need to spend so much. In a historic review of U.S. defense forces, Clinton's former secretary of defense, Les Aspin, said that "the framework that guided our security policy during the Cold War is inadequate for the future."

Citing a "potential failure to build a strong and growing U.S. economy" as one of the four key threats facing America in the post–Cold War era, Aspin called for a shift of resources "to meet the dangers to American . . . prosperity and seize the opportunity to accelerate U.S. economic growth."

The cost of a wrong-size military is staggering:

- A single B-2 bomber would buy 424 new elementary schools for 254,000 children.

- Rather than buying 21 additional Trident II missiles, we could provide prenatal care for 2,127,000 low-income mothers.

- For less than the cost of one Aegis destroyer, 263,374 preschoolers could be enrolled in Head Start for one year.

To ensure that our generation and those to follow have a strong military and a strong economic future, we must slowly reduce military spending to $200 billion by the year 2000.

This is an achievable goal. We can make these cuts and still sustain a strong military. Compare our

"With a 25 percent cut in our defense spending, America can sustain the most powerful military in the world, the most potent air force in existence, a navy with no rival, and the most lethal nuclear arsenal on the planet."
—Robert Borosage, defense expert, Campaign for New Priorities

streamlined forces to those used in Desert
Storm.

Forces	Forces Used in DS	Our Option
Army Divisions	8	22
Marine Corps Brigades	6	11
Air Force Fighter Wings	10	22
Carrier Battle Groups	6	9

Defense experts from the highly respected
Brookings Institution and the Center for
Defense Information agree that by spending
$200 billion a year on the military the U.S.
would still be able to fulfill effectively all of its
core military missions with only one change:
Our allies would have to take on a fair share of
their own defense.

This proposal is endorsed by the Campaign for New Priorities, a
national effort to enlist citizen support for a new set of budget priorities, by the National Rainbow Coalition, a progressive political
organization that advocates for a new set of humane, domestic priorities, and by 20/20 Vision, a grass-roots group of 10,000 members fighting on environmental and peace issues. To find out more
about some of the new choices our nation can consider, call:

20/20 Vision   (202) 833-2020
The Campaign for New Priorities   (202) 544-8222
The National Rainbow Coalition   (202) 728-1180

This is a worthwhile tradeoff for America even if the former Soviet Union reemerges as a threat. Japan and Germany have the economic might to provide for their own defense. The United Nations provides an additional safety blanket, and we can still maintain a ready force to help defend our allies should that ever be necessary.

This scaled-down force structure—put in place gradually over the next six years—would provide us with the capability of meeting our national security needs and at the same time free up resources to invest in our people and our technology base and to provide fiscal stability by lowering our deficit.

It's time to "right-size" America's military. America has a historic opportunity to scale back our military spending *without* jeopardizing our defense. We should take it.

CHALLENGE #7 MAKE EDUCATION
AFFORDABLE

PROBLEM: The high cost of attending college, combined with rising tuition levels and huge loan repayment costs, has put higher education out of reach for millions of Americans.

SOLUTION: Given the high returns in productivity and taxes from college-
educated citizens, the federal
government should make college
affordable for everyone.

In 1944, President Franklin Roosevelt
signed into law the Servicemen's Readjustment
Act—better known as the G.I. Bill. The act
ensured that millions of servicemen and service-
women, coming home from World War II,
would get the education they needed to launch
productive careers.

At the peak of the program in 1949, the price
tag on the G.I. Bill was $2.7 billion—or 1 per-
cent of the 1949 GNP. Today the
investment is widely credited with
making possible the dramatic ex-
pansion of America's middle class.
Never since has our country so
badly needed to make a similar
investment in younger Americans.

After purchase of a home, a college education is ranked as the second largest cost in the life of an
American family, and polls show
that many younger Americans and
their families no longer believe they
can afford the cost of college.

That shouldn't be the case. In
1965, with the passage of the
Higher Education Act, the federal

"I went to one of the
best colleges in the
United States and I'm
working as a bike
messenger for next to
nothing, no benefits,
barely paying my rent,
not paying my college
loans."
—Eben, 25-year-old
graphic designer

government reiterated its commitment to invest in future generations, accepting a federal responsibility to eliminate financial barriers
to higher education.

Despite Washington's commitment, current federal student aid
and loan programs fail to meet the
rising costs of earning a degree and
the financial needs of most students
and their families. What's more, current federal assistance programs fail
to provide adequate resources to
the emerging majority of "nontradi-
tional" students—minorities, older students, single parents, and part-time and evening students.

> Between 1980 and
> 1990 the total cost of
> attending a private
> college increased by
> 146 percent. The total
> level of assistance
> (federal, state, and
> institutional) increased
> by less than half that.

In addition, high debt repayment costs (the
average cost of a four-year degree is $56,000)
overwhelm the budgets of many graduates and
prevent them from choosing community service
jobs or careers in public life.

In 1993, a presidentially and congressionally
appointed national commission charged with
exploring new ways to finance higher education
developed the STEP Plan. STEP—which stands
for the Student Total Education Package—is a
major reform program to unify the entire federal
aid system and change the way many Americans
pay for college. STEP was the federal government's admission that the current programs are
inadequate and an attempt to solve the crisis in
higher education funding before the next century.

According to the Association of Big Ten Schools, Stafford Loans, the largest federally backed loan program, serve only one in three college students at the Big Ten schools.

Under the STEP plan, every student would be eligible for the average yearly cost of attending college—estimated in 1993 at $14,000. The federal government would ensure access to this amount for every student through a combination of grants, work-study, and subsidized and unsubsidized loans, depending on the income of the student and his or her family.

In other words, the type of aid would differ—based on need and cost of attendance—but everyone would be ensured a minimum level of resources to attend college. A college education would become a real opportunity for all younger Americans.

Here's how it would work: A lower-income student would receive a federal aid package made up mostly of grants, work-study, and subsidized loans, while a middle-income student would have fewer grants and more loans. Upper-income students would receive no grants, but would be eligible for the same amount of assistance in unsubsidized loans.

STEP will cost the federal government only an additional $7 billion a year. In return, it will ensure that no student misses out on a college education because of financial need. STEP also will allow students to know in advance (based on the unified formula) exactly how much assistance—and what types—they can expect to receive from the federal government.

It's also a good investment. For every dollar of federal assistance, the U.S. government earns an average return of $4.50 in future tax receipts. The federal government should lead the way in establishing a compact to make higher education affordable for all Americans. STEP is the right first step.

Like the G.I. Bill 50 years ago, the STEP plan will allow millions of younger Americans to get badly needed training and education to secure their economic futures, earn their way into the middle class, and provide a growing tax base to actually pay for the baby boom retirement.

This type of program would make education more affordable for low- and middle-income students and their families, ensure a fairer distribution of total aid resources, and unify the currently complex and uncertain system of federal grants and aid. It's good politics and good policy.

This proposal is endorsed by the Association of Big Ten Schools (ABTS) and the National Coalition for Student Empowerment.

To find out more about how to make higher education affordable and fiscally sound for both our generation and all of America, or to find out more about other issues of concern to students, contact an ABTS director via student government at any Big Ten School, or call:

National Coalition for Student Empowerment (602) 621-2782
Association of Big Ten Schools (310) 337-9605

CHALLENGE #8 GIVE EQUAL RIGHTS TO GAYS

PROBLEM: Gay people face legal discrimination throughout America.

SOLUTION: Pass a federal law to protect all
Americans from discrimination
based on sexual orientation.

Every day in America people are fired from
their jobs, kicked out of their apartments, and
denied public services solely because of their sexual orientation. It may be surprising, but no federal law protects gay Americans from discrimination, and only a handful of states
give gay people the same protection
provided to other Americans.

"Discrimination against
gays is just as need-
less, just as hurtful, just
as damaging to those
it affects as all other
forms of discrimina-
tion. Let's face it,
there's nothing very
positive in being a
bigot."
—Tom, 28-year-old
    former journalist

The story of Cheryl Summer-
ville is just one example. Cheryl
was a short-order cook at a
Cracker Barrel restaurant outside
Atlanta, Georgia. She worked for
several years and had a great job
record with the restaurant chain
before they issued a new policy
requiring managers to fire their gay
and lesbian employees.

Cheryl lost her job, her home,
and her insurance. Without protection under Georgia or federal law,
there was nothing she could do.

Polls consistently show that a majority of Americans oppose discrimination against gay people. It's especially true for our generation. A *Newsweek* poll in early 1994 found that young people were consistently more supportive of ending discrimination on the basis of sexual orientation than was any other age group.

Despite public opposition, an organized minority and a lot of indifference have allowed anti-gay discrimination to remain legal in 42 states.

As young Americans, whether gay or not, we can work for all Americans to be treated fairly. Coretta Scott King put it this way: "I believe all Americans who believe in freedom, tolerance, and human rights have a responsibility to oppose bigotry and prejudice based on sexual orientation."

This proposal is backed by the Human Rights Campaign Fund, the largest gay and lesbian political organization in America. To find out more about ending discrimination and how everyone in our generation can help stop it, call:

Human Rights Campaign Fund   (202) 628-4160

Discrimination, no matter who it's against, is un-American and benefits no one. Congress should enact federal legislation to eliminate job discrimination based on sexual orientation.

CHALLENGE #9 HELP END HOMELESSNESS

PROBLEM: There are 7 million homeless in America.

SOLUTION: Aggressively fund homeless programs to help children and the next generation of workers.

While most of us may offer up a little change or just step over the homeless, their presence is a symbol of the social decay that has overtaken America in the last 20 years. As we now know, many of the homeless are children—some estimate there are 1.7 million to 2 million homeless children in America (imagine a city the size of Atlanta, Denver, or Saint Louis filled entirely with homeless kids).

What did these children do to deserve being cast aside by their country? Nothing, of course, except have the bad luck of being born into disadvantaged families, many of whom lost decent-paying jobs and were forced out of public housing and onto the streets.

As homeless expert and author Jonathan Kozol writes, "In Portland, Oregon, the governor told

"I used to be homeless; now I run a shelter and hold office. The homeless shouldn't be treated like trash; they're good people who need another chance."
—Keith Mitchell, executive director, Community for Creative Non-Violence

me of some counties in which unemployment caused by the declining lumber industry had climbed above 30 percent. Where did the lumber workers go? . . . A homeless shelter by the Burnside Bridge."

If we are going to give our children and poor families a fair chance, we're going to have to aggressively fund homeless programs to break this cycle. In a 1994 report released by President Clinton's secretary of housing and urban development, the secretary endorsed an outstanding proposal for funding such programs, which could bring in billions. His idea: Scale back the tax deduction for mortgage interest available to wealthy home-owners and devote some of this money to support more subsidized housing, mental health facilities, and other effective programs.

This proposal is backed by two groups leading the fight to solve the homeless problem:

National Student Campaign Against Hunger and Homelessness
(617) 292-4823
Community for Creative Non-Violence
(202) 393-1909

Currently, evey home owner is allowed to deduct from his taxes the amount of interest he pays on his home loan—a subsidy that was designed years ago to encourage home ownership.

If that subsidy were withheld from people with homes worth more than $250,000, only 5 percent of America's 27 million home owners would be affected—and billions of dollars would be freed up to provide badly needed assistance to low-income families and homeless children.

It's a fair and economically sound trade-off for all Americans.

CHALLENGE #10 GUARANTEE FREEDOM
OF CHOICE

PROBLEM: A determined minority seeks to make abortion illegal.

SOLUTION: Pass federal legislation ensuring long-term protection for a woman's right to choose.

> "It makes me sick to think of politicians making decisions about my body. I doubt choice will ever be totally secure."
> —Jenny, 25-year-old congressional aide

Many in our generation, raised after the historic *Roe versus Wade* decision, have never known a time when women were routinely forced into the back alleys to obtain abortions. Yet even in the 1990s, reproductive services are becoming increasingly difficult to obtain for many women, particularly young and poor women.

Today, only 17 percent of American counties have even one medical provider willing to perform abortions. Most women must travel significant distances to obtain services. Many clinics are picketed daily or weekly. And there have been over a thousand violent incidents at clinics, including firebombings, arsons, acid attacks, invasions, and shootings, since the early 1980s.

States across America have enacted laws requiring women to wait 24 hours before having an abortion once they've arrived at the clinic. These laws wrongly assume that women make this difficult personal choice on impulse and must be sent home to think about it first.

Anti-choice forces have been stymied in their efforts to overturn *Roe* outright, but the combined effects of such state restriction, anti-choice violence, and the shortage of providers place "freedom of choice" at risk in the coming decades.

To guarantee that right, Washington should pass the Freedom of Choice Act, now pending before Congress. While not a comprehensive solution, passage would prevent the imposition of waiting periods and would be one important step in permanently securing the right to choose for women of all generations.

This proposal is endorsed by the National Abortion and Reproductive Rights Action League, a leading voice for women's reproductive rights. To become a member of NARAL, or to find out more about your rights or reproductive services available to you, call:

National Abortion and Reproductive Rights Action League   (202) 973-3000

CHALLENGE #11 TRIM AMERICA'S BUDGET

PROBLEM: Washington squanders billions of your tax dollars every year to fund outdated and unnecessary programs.

SOLUTION: Trim Uncle Sam's bloated budget.

From useless weapons systems to unused veterans' hospitals, the federal budget is bursting with ineffective or unneeded programs.

"The government sucks from the public trough."
—Ellen, 29-year-old legal secretary

Despite tough talk about performance reviews and government reinvention, we have yet to see the kind of real budgetary cuts that would permanently downsize Washington—and save us billions.

What follows is a congressional budget-cutter's start-up kit.

Step 1. Wipe Out 34 Ineffective Programs

In the Concord Coalition's Zero Deficit Plan released last year, Senators Paul Tsongas and Warren Rudman call for the elimination or reduction of 50 government programs that are either not working, not necessary, or no longer affordable, or that subsidize narrow special interests. *Eliminating just two-thirds of these would save taxpayers almost $20 billion by the year 2000.*

What programs would we reduce and/or eliminate? Subsidies to AMTRAK and the Rural Electrification Administration, the space station, highway demonstration projects, subsidies that go to harvest timber from our national forests or to lower postal rates for not-for-profit organizations, and spending on underused VA hospitals.

> "The government should spend money on things that any nation has to spend money on—defense, a social safety net, critical government operations. But too often spending isn't used to address a *real* need or a need that benefits the whole nation. That's the waste we can get rid of."
> —Bob, 28-year-old systems analyst

Step 2. Reform Federal Pensions

Fortune 500 versus Uncle Sam. When it comes to total pension compensation, there's no contest. Federal workers get twice what their pri-

vate sector counterparts get—more even than
lifetime employees of Fortune 500 companies.

We can save almost $6 billion in the year
2000 alone, and more in the following years,
by changing the way we calculate pensions and
eliminating cost-of-living increases for nondis-
abled retirees younger than 62—giving them
instead a one-time catch-up increase after they
turn 65.

Step 3. Cut Administrative Spending by
5 Percent

The federal government is more than a payroll.
It's a giant corporation with all kinds of operating expenses. But because the government has
no bottom line, it can run some pretty staggering overhead.

Surprisingly, the government doesn't keep
track of its actual overhead costs—rent, phones,
photocopying, travel, and decorating, to name a
few—but the Office of Management and Budget
puts the figure as high as $270 billion a year. *A
5 percent cut in overhead would generate $14
billion to $17 billion a year in savings.*

Step 4. Eliminate Half a Million
Civil Service Jobs

With over 2.2 million federal jobs, the annual
price tag for the federal payroll is over $113 bil-

Citizens Against Government Waste (CAGW), which endorses this package of spending cuts, is a 600,000-member, private, nonprofit, nonpartisan organization dedicated to educating the American public about waste, mismanagement, and inefficiency in the federal government. Call:

Citizens Against Government Waste   (202) 467-5300

lion—and that doesn't count retirement pensions and benefits.

Every year, 7 percent of the federal work force leaves, retires, or dies. Even if we rehired 20 percent of the lost jobs—more than enough to ensure that all critical positions remain filled—by the year 2000 we could eliminate 550,000 federal jobs and save over $100 billion in salaries, benefits, and future pensions without firing a single person.

How much would we save? Forty-six billion dollars in the year 2000 alone.

The bottom line: Add up all these cuts and you'd save about $80 billion annually by the year 2000—without taking a dime away from the needy or jeopardizing any essential government services.

CHALLENGE #12 WIN AFFORDABLE
HEALTH CARE

PROBLEM: While the 1990s are likely to see the adoption of universal health care coverage, most proposed plans would finance this new coverage by unfunded taxes on future generations.

SOLUTION: Any fair health care reform must include a "youth-friendly" financing mechanism that is based on your ability to pay, not your age or your benefit level.

Millions of younger Americans stand to benefit greatly from universal coverage, since many of the uninsured are under the age of 35. America's economy also stands to benefit since reined-in health care costs will lower the deficit. But we must be careful that today's health reform does not become tomorrow's runaway entitlement program. That's what happened 30 years ago with Medicare.

In 1965, the first year President Lyndon Johnson offered Medicare (providing health coverage for all

> "If I got hit by a car I'd be better off if I died because I couldn't afford the hospital bill anyway."
> —Eve, 28-year-old student

seniors), the program cost less than $50 million—and the U.S. government predicted a total cost of less than $10 billion by 1990.

They were wrong, way wrong. The program actually cost us almost $110 billion in 1990 (nearly 11 times what was originally predicted), and it's still growing. In 1965, the payroll tax that finances Medicare was one-third of 1 percent of a person's salary. If you earned $21,000 (a lot back then), you would have paid just $70. Today that's increased more than eightfold. You would pay almost $600—and that covers just *half* of the real costs of Medicare. In other words, for every dollar spent on Medicare, the U.S. goes 50 cents deeper into debt.

Soon, the situation will get a lot worse. The Social Security and Medicare boards of trustees have warned that the primary Medicare trust fund will go bankrupt by the year 2000, or earlier. At that point, the government will have to raise taxes dramatically to cover the benefit demand, or it will stop writing checks to retirees.

As Washington considers some form of universal health care coverage, younger Americans must fight to ensure that expanded coverage is paid for in a way that is fair to all generations and does not drive up the debt. Right now, the burden of financing the new health care system, no matter which plan passes, falls most heavily on younger, poorer workers.

The less you make, the bigger the tax bur-

den. That's how Social Security is currently
financed. A thirtysomething family with two
kids making $45,000 a year pays over 15 per-
cent of their salary to fund Social Security; a
billionaire pays less than 1 percent of his earnings. That is unfair and unwise budget policy,
driven not by smart economics but by the political fear that the powerful senior lobbies will
use their muscle to block reform if retirees are
asked to pay a higher share.

If reform is going to be fair and workable
for years to come, this "give-it-to-me-free" attitude is a recipe for disaster. There is no free
lunch. If America wants universal coverage,
Washington is going to have to ask everybody
(except the poor) to pay something. The more
you make, the more you're going to have to
pay. It's that simple.

It's income, not age, that must determine
how much you pay in health care taxes. If
it's fair for a 25-year-old who works at
McDonald's to pay more, than it's fair for a
wealthy 75-year-old—who will get additional
benefits from reform—to pay more as well.

This proposal was researched and designed by Lead . . . or Leave.
For more detailed information on how health care reform affects
younger voters, or to become a member, please contact Rock the
Vote, an organization that has registered thousands of new voters
and helped win passage of the Motor Voter bill.

Rock the Vote   (310) 441-2581

A "Youth-Friendly" Plan

Specifically, we propose a two-step plan that would keep the system solvent over the long run and be equitable to all generations:

1. Eliminate any cap on the health care portion of payroll taxes. That means everyone pays the tax on all of their salary. Whether you make $25,000 a year, $2 million, or $50 million, you pay the health care tax on every dollar you earn.

2. Place a health care surtax on the income (all investments, retirement funds, etc.) of retirees making $100,000 or more a year. Why a surtax on cash income? Most retirees don't pay payroll taxes (since they no longer collect a "salary"), so under most health care proposals, wealthy retirees would be exempt from paying for their benefits.

CHALLENGE #13 REFORM OUR POLITICS

PROBLEM: Washington is a mess.

SOLUTION: Crack down on perks and the abuse of power.

Every two years, Washington pledges to clean itself up, yet new scandals are always

> "Many members of Congress avail themselves of a swank and luxurious lifestyle filled with epicurean meals and posh vacations paid for by special-interest lobbyists. This is how lobbyists facilitate their influence on votes."
>
> —Ralph Nader, citizen activist and founder of Public Citizen

emerging: S&L corruption, midnight salary hikes, check bouncing, runaway deficits, $500 toilet seats, Iran-Contra.

Members of Congress take millions in political action committee (PAC) money and on top of that are treated to "working" trips to Florida spas and Utah ski resorts, paid for by corporate lobbyists. Is it any wonder that we have an endless stream of special-interest subsidies—$800,000 for a bathroom on Mount McKinley, $2.7 million for an Arkansas catfish farm, $33 million for sand on private beaches?

Figure this out: President Bush's fiscal 1993 travel budget was $100,000, but Air Force One's estimated hourly operating cost is $40,233. That would allow the president to travel for three hours a year. In other words, the White House hid the real costs of travel in other budget categories, hoping to shrink the public size of the president's "travel budget." (Unfortunately, wherever the costs are buried, we still pay.)

As Vice President Al Gore said in his national performance review, "The federal government has grown stale, wasteful, inefficient, bureaucratic, and is failing the American people."

The ultimate success of any 1990s citizen movement rests on our ability to hold our political leaders accountable to coming generations—and that means we must clean up Washington. Following are some of the key changes that would help make Washington work for us.

- Provide public funding for all federal elections—barring candidates who took private donations, even from themselves or their families, from receiving one dime of public money.

- Congress must be covered by every law it passes, and its members should receive the same kind of treatment (health care, pension benefits, parking, travel) available to the average American.

- Limit congressional pensions so that they are on a par with private pensions. Former vice president Dan Quayle, who is heir to a multi-million-dollar family newspaper fortune, is expected to collect $1.8 million in retirement benefits in his lifetime, starting at age 60.

- Create a presidentially appointed Commission on Perks that would eliminate all special favors to Congress and the White House.

- Shut the revolving door by prohibiting former congressmen who are registered lobbyists from using their "floor privileges," which give retired members full access to the floor of the House or Senate. Bar former members of Congress and their high-ranking staff from lobbying for five years after leaving office, and do the same for high-ranking executive branch officials. Prohibit all former top-level executive branch officials from ever becoming foreign agents.

■ Prohibit members of Congress and their staff from accepting any donations, however small, from registered lobbyists.

This package of reforms has been endorsed by Public Citizen, one of the nation's leading consumer and advocacy organizations, founded by Ralph Nader in 1970. To receive more information on election and congressional reform, or to join the 150,000 members of Public Citizen, call:

Public Citizen   (202) 546-4996

CHAPTER 7

CHOOSING OUR FATE

A GENERATION AWARE and involved will do more for the country than a generation trapped in apathy. We are more likely to see an end to the toxic policies of the last few decades if we are part of a larger movement to define a new agenda and fight for its passage.

The battle is well under way. Networks are forming and coalitions are building. Across the country, people who care are joining together to make a difference. Groups are linking up, setting up clearinghouses, and establishing a mandate for generational change.

A unique combination of factors—economic, political, and demographic—has created an environment in which a new generation can help guide the country toward economic and social renewal. The reasons for a new era of activism are compelling.

> "The first thing you have to do is get up off the couch and stop watching television. You have to be about something."
> —Shannon Reeves, 24-year-old director of the NAACP West Coast regional office

- Our generation is bound by a common interest: a concern for our economic security and our nation's well-being.

- We have the numbers to be a powerful and effective activist force.

- We have the most potential to change politics in America. Many of us care—and are ready to fight back.

We have already waited too long for our leaders to rebuild our crumbling cities, reorder our national priorities, and start making wise choices about how we spend our country's money. Why wait any longer? Why hope for a miracle that will not come?

There are solutions to the enormous challenges facing our generation, but they will only be found if each of us invests some effort in the process of defining and defending a new agenda for America.

True, there's an opportunity cost; time spent volunteering, voting, and voicing your opinions is time you don't have to watch TV, read a book, go to the gym, take a dance class, or hang out with friends.

But while becoming more active today might seem to conflict with your job, your classes, your social life, it's a small cost for the change you will help create—a small price to pay for the privilege of living in the greatest nation on earth.

If you sit out the game, someone else will decide the rules for you. Someone else will decide how to spend your taxes. Someone else will decide what you can do with your body, how much money to give out in student loans, what kind of environment your children will inherit.

How many homeless people does our generation have to step over and ignore before we decide—together—that we should work to put an end to homelessness?

How many more times do we have to turn on C-SPAN or flip through *Time* magazine before deciding that Congressman X (who has been in Washington since before we were born) has outlived his welcome?

How many dead-end jobs will we hold, how big a bite do taxes have to take out of our lives, how many times does a friend have to get mugged before we decide that America's decline is going to cost us personally—and must be turned around?

VOICES OF A NEW GENERATION

It is not for our generation to let our future slip away from us, to stand by as the politicians mortgage our country. We are called to this fight against political expediency not by guilt or shame, but by pride in what we have been and can be as a nation. We are called to speak out, each of us, by our rights and responsibilities as citizens.

We are called to take this action because to do less would be to forsake the very thing that makes us American. If we turn away, we lose more than our economic strength and social dignity; we lose the strength of our convictions, the purpose of our powerful nation.

Revolution by evolution doesn't require any of us to radically reorder our lives. We don't need to quit our jobs and take to the streets in protest. A small measure of commitment from each of us will add up to a powerful new force for change—a generation called to action, a generation prepared to defend our country and our future.

In the life of any democracy that hopes to endure, there come times when the people must take up tasks of repair and renewal—*when the people must lead and the "leaders" follow.*

For America the time has once again come to initiate a shift as profound as that which occurred in any of the other revolutionary moments in our history—as dramatic as proclaiming that there should be no more slavery, that separate white and black schools are neither equal nor just, and that women must be given the right to vote.

It *is* possible to rebuild this nation, stop spending what we don't have, and start giving our generation a decent chance. We can stop the spread of AIDS, mend our broken cities, put a choke collar on crime, and make our political system more responsive to citizens and their needs.

But we can't change America from our living room couches.

If we all hope to have a bright future, we must each devote some meaningful measure of our time to restoring the integrity of our nation's politics and forcing our leaders to make one simple choice.

> "There are some really tough times, but when you can get through them, it's such a great accomplishment or a feeling of surviving."
> —Mary, 28-year-old executive assistant

Do the right thing for future generations, or be booted out of office.

What if we do nothing? Imagine our generation preparing a time capsule on the first day of the year 2000, setting it to open 50 years later on December 31, 2049. Sealed inside is a single document, a letter to our children and grandchildren. It reads:

"Dear kids,

"We're sorry about the $20 trillion national debt, the collapse of the Social Security system, the hollowed-out inner cities, the unbreathable air, our third-rate economic status, and your 70 percent tax rates.

"We know that many of you cannot afford to buy homes, lack adequate health coverage, and will never be able to send your kids to college. We're ashamed that we've put you in a situation where a lack of resources will force you to choose between the needs of the young and the old—a choice no society should ever have to make.

"You probably wonder how this happened. You must want an explanation, some kind of justification. We cannot offer one.

"No foreign power descended on our soil taking our ideals hostage. No outside force compelled us to mortgage our country. We did this to ourselves. We did it of our own free will. And we did it knowing the consequences to our children and grandchildren.

"We saw what was coming but we continued to hide out in our homes, our neighborhoods, and our universities, unable to face the real impact of our apathy. Book after book, study after study sounded the warning. We put the books on the bestseller list, but we did not put the warnings into action.

"Instead, we squandered your inheritance, which had been acquired at great cost and passed on from one generation to the next throughout American history.

"In living so far beyond our means, we

have seriously compromised your standard
of living and that of all generations of
Americans to come after you. We apologize.
We didn't mean to hurt you. We just didn't
do what we could."

Today the fate of our generation is *our*
choice. We can stand by while America collapses on our watch, or we can redeem our
national purpose and dignity—putting our
economy back on course, embracing a new
form of grass-roots democracy, and pressuring
our leaders for a radical revision of our politics.

If you turn away, thinking that by acting
alone none of us can succeed, your inaction
makes it all the more likely that we all will fail.
But if each of us makes a commitment, however small or large, to get more involved today,
our individual acts will be magnified, and the
collective impact will change our nation.

We do not have to follow in our parents'
footsteps. Where they have rejected sacrifice,
we can embrace national renewal.

Where they have been content with business
as usual from Washington, we can agitate for
real reform.

Where they have remained divided and fear-
ful, we can draw together across racial and
class lines.

Where they have looked to the next election, we can set our sights on the next generation.

We have been silent for too long. Our voices must now be heard. Our votes must now be counted. America's future hangs in the balance, and our future hangs with America's.

If we do not respond, the fate of our democracy—and of each of our lives—is sealed. We do not have the luxury of waiting another year, another season, for visionary or courageous politicians to emerge. They have had their chance; now we must seize ours.

AN ACTION KIT

CONTENTS

USING THE ACTION KIT

During the last couple years, many people have asked us for help in becoming more active: how to find out more about issues, which political and community service organizations to join, and how to learn more about the tools for action—from using the Internet and registering to vote to tapping into alternative media.

While the ultimate solution is some type of a generational activism clearinghouse, we thought this action guide would make a good first step. We've included several hundred advocacy and community-service organizations, a listing of the top alternative media (including E-Mail addresses where available), a guide to using the Internet, information on voter registration, and the phone numbers and addresses of state and national leaders.

We have also put together a collection of the

100 harshest facts facing our generation, and an extensive listing of books, magazines, and articles that we used in writing this book. There is a lot of core information to be used as a springboard for anyone who wants to dive a little deeper.

So here's your Action Kit. It can be useful to beginners as well as to people who are already activists. There are no rules about getting involved—except that you have to start somewhere and you are never really finished. Hopefully this guide will help you along the way.

I: GETTING INVOLVED

We've listed several hundred advocacy, community action, and research organizations. Many are run by our generation (we've listed these in bold type), and all of them are doing important work.

There are thousands of other organizations doing worthwhile things, but we couldn't include all of them. Instead, we tried to get a diverse and representative list of groups, and include those that we think are having the most impact.

ORGANIZATIONS

(Organizations in bold are specially geared toward younger people.)

African American

Black Student Leadership Network
25 E Street NW
Washington, D.C. 20001
(202) 628-8787

Martin Luther King Jr. Center for Non-Violent Social Change
449 Auburn Ave.
Atlanta, GA 30312
(404) 524-1956

NAACP National Headquarters
4805 Mount Hope Dr.
Baltimore, MD 21215-3297
(410) 358-8900

**NAACP Youth and College
Division**
4805 Mount Hope Dr.
Baltimore, MD 21215-3297
(410) 358-8900 ext. 9134

National Urban League, Inc.
500 East 62nd St.
New York, NY 10021
(212) 310-9000

Southern Christian Leadership
Conference
334 Auburn Ave. NE
Atlanta, GA 30303
(404) 522-1420

United Black Fund, Inc.
1101 14th St. NW, 6th Floor
Washington, D.C. 20005
(202) 783-9300

Children

Big Brothers/Big Sisters of
America
230 North 13th St.
Philadelphia, PA 19107
(215) 567-7000

Children's Defense Fund
25 E. St. NW
Washington, D.C. 20001
(202) 628-8787

Children's Express
30 Cooper Square, 4th Floor
New York, NY 10003
(212) 505-7777

Generations Together
University of Pittsburgh
121 University Place, Suite 300
Pittsburgh, PA 15260-5907
(412) 648-7150

Crime

Coalition to Stop Gun Violence
100 Maryland Ave. NE
Suite 402
Washington, D.C. 20002
(202) 544-7190

Handgun Control
1225 Eye St.
Washington, D.C. 20005
(202) 898-0792

National Association of Town
Watch
P.O. Box 303
Wynnewood, PA 19096
(215) 649-7055

National Crime Prevention
Council
1700 K St. NW, 2nd Floor
Washington, D.C. 20006
(202) 466-6272

Safe Streets Now!
408 13th St., Suite 452
Oakland, CA 94612
(510) 836-4622

Economy

American Enterprise Institute for
Public Policy Research
1150 17th St. NW, #1100
Washington, D.C. 20036
(202) 862-5800

Campaign for New Priorities
424 C St. NW, Basement
Washington, D.C. 20002
(202) 544-8222

Center for Defense Information
1500 Massachusetts Ave. NW
Washington, D.C. 20005
(202) 862-0700

Center for National Policy
1 Massachusetts Ave. NW
Suite 333
Washington, D.C. 20001
(202) 682-1800

Center for Policy Alternatives
1875 Connecticut Ave. NW
#710
Washington, D.C. 20009
(202) 387-6030

Committee for a Responsible
Federal Budget
220 1/2 E St. NE
Washington, D.C. 20002
(202) 547-4484

Committee for Economic
Development
2000 L St. NW, #700
Washington, D.C. 20036
(202) 296-5860

Concord Coalition
1025 Vermont Ave. NW, #810
Washington, D.C. 20005
(202) 737-1077

Council on Competitiveness
900 17th St. NW, #1050
Washington, D.C. 20006
(202) 785-3990

Defense Budget Project
777 N. Capitol St. NE, #710
Washington, D.C. 20002
(202) 408-1517

Economic Policy Institute
1730 Rhode Island Ave. NW
#200
Washington, D.C. 20036
(202) 775-8810

Hudson Institute
1015 18th St. NW, #200
Washington, D.C. 20036
(202) 223-7770

Progressive Policy Institute
518 C St. NE
Washington, D.C. 20002
(202) 547-0001

Education

D.A.R.E.
P.O. Box 2090
Los Angeles, CA 90051-0090
(800) 223-3273

Literacy Volunteers of America
5795 Widewaters Parkway
Syracuse, NY 13214
(315) 445-8000

Names Project Foundation
310 Townsend St., Suite 310
San Francisco, CA 94107
(415) 882-5500

New School for Social Research
66 West 12th St.
New York, NY 10011
(212) 229-5600

Student Pugwash, USA
1638 R St. NW, Suite 32
Washington, D.C. 20009-6446
(202) 328-6555

United States Student Association
815 15th St. NW, Suite 838
Washington, D.C. 20005
(202) 347-USSA

Unplug
360 Grand Ave., Box 385
Oakland, CA 94610
(510) 268-1100
(800) UNPLUG1

Empowerment

100% Vote/Human Serve
622 W. 113 St., Suite 410
New York, NY 10025
(212) 854-4053

ACORN
739 8th St. SE
Washington, D.C. 20003
(202) 547-9292

Advocacy Institute
1730 Rhode Island Ave. NW
Suite 600
Washington, D.C. 20036-3118
(202) 659-8475

Center for Community Change
1000 Wisconsin Ave. NW
Washington, D.C. 20007
(202) 342-0519

Detroit Summer
4605 Class Ave.
Detroit, MI 48202
(313) 832-2904

Get IT Together
1436 U St. NW
Washington, D.C. 20009

Global Kids
New York Alliance for the Public
Schools
561 Broadway, 6th Floor
New York, NY 10012
(212) 226-0130

Grace Contrino Abrams Peace
Education
2627 Biscayne Blvd.
Miami, FL 33137
(800) 749-8838

Independent Sector
1828 L St. NW, #1200
Washington, D.C. 20036
(202) 223-8100

Leadership Initiative Project
c/o Angela Brown & Kim Burwell
Rt. 1, Box 119
Kitrell, NC 27544
(919) 437-0319

Midwest Academy
225 West Ohio, Suite 250
Chicago, IL 60610
(312) 645-6010

National Rainbow Coalition, Inc.
1700 K St. NW, Suite 800
Washington, D.C. 20006
(202) 728-1180

Project Public Life
Humphrey Center
301 19th Ave. South
Minneapolis, MN 55455
(612) 625-9505

Project Vote
739 8th St. SE, Suite 202
Washington, D.C. 20003
(202) 546-3492

Southern Community Partners
P.O. Box 19745
North Carolina Central
University
Durham, NC 27707
(919) 683-1840

Voter Research Hotline
129 North West 4th St.
Suite 204
Corvallis, OR 97330
(800) 622-SMART

Environment

20/20 Vision Project
1828 Jefferson Pl. NW
Washington, D.C. 20036
(202) 833-2020

Activists Concerned with Toxics
in Our Neighborhoods
1080 U.S. 22 West
P.O. Box 67
Circleville, OH 43113
(614) 474-1240

Californians Against Waste
Foundation
926 J St., Suite 606
Sacramento, CA 95814
(916) 443-5422

Campus Green Vote
1400 16th St. NW
Washington, D.C. 20036

Champaign Park District
706 Kenwood Rd.
Champaign, IL 61821
(217) 398-2550

**Circle of Indigenous
Youth/Indigenous Environmental
Network**
P.O. Box 701796
Tulsa, OK 74170

Cool It! and Endangered Species
Campaign
National Wildlife Federation
1400 16th St. NW
Washington, D.C. 20036-2266
(202) 797-6800

Defenders of Wildlife
1101 14th St. NW, Suite 1400
Washington, D.C. 20005
(202) 682-9400

Earth Force
1501 Wilson Blvd., 12th Floor
Arlington, VA 22209
(703) 243-6999

Earthwatch
680 Mount Auburn St., Box 403
Watertown, MA 02172
(617) 926-8200

Ecomedia
926 N St. NW
Washington, D.C. 20001
(202) 842-3577

Friends of the Earth
1025 Vermont Ave. NW
Washington, D.C. 20003
(202) 783-7400

Green Corps
37 Temple Pl.
Boston, MA 02111
(617) 426-8506

Greenpeace
1436 U St. NW, #305
Washington, D.C. 20009
(202) 462-1177

League of Conservation Voters
1707 L St. NW, #550
Washington, D.C. 20036
(202) 785-8683

National Audubon Society
666 Pennsylvania Ave. SE, #200
Washington, D.C. 20003
(202) 547-9009

Natural Resources Defense
Council
1350 New York Ave. NW, #300
Washington, D.C. 20005
(202) 783-7800

Renew America
1400 16th St. NW, #710
Washington, D.C. 20036
(202) 232-2252

Sierra Club
730 Polk St.
San Francisco, CA 94109
(415) 776-2211

Southwest Network for
Environmental and Economic
Justice
P.O. Box 7399
Albuquerque, NM 87194
(505) 242-0416

**Student Environmental Action
Coalition**
P.O. Box 1168
Chapel Hill, NC 27514
(919) 967-4600
(800) 700-SEAC

World Wildlife Fund and
Conservation Foundation
1250 24th St. NW, #400
Washington, D.C. 20037
(202) 293-4800

Worldwatch Institute
1776 Massachusetts Ave., NW
8th Floor
Washington, D.C. 20036
(202) 452-1999

Youth for Environmental Sanity!
706 Fredrick St.
Santa Cruz, CA 95062

Gay/Lesbian

ACLU Lesbian and Gay Rights
Project
132 W. 43rd St.
New York, NY 10036
(212) 944-9800

Human Rights Campaign Fund
1101 14th St. NW, 2nd Floor
Washington, D.C. 20005
(202) 628-4160

National Gay and Lesbian Task
Force
2320 17th St. NW
Washington, D.C. 20009
(202) 332-6483

Queer Nation
P.O. Box 34773
Washington, D.C. 20043
(301) 294-4358

Health

ACT-UP
135 W. 29th St., 10th Floor
New York, NY 10001
(212) 564-2437

AIDS Action Council
1875 Connecticut Ave., NW
Suite 700
Washington, D.C. 20009
(202) 986-1300

Planned Parenthood Federation of
America
810 7th Ave.
New York, NY 10019
(212) 541-7800

San Francisco AIDS Foundation
25 Van Ness Ave., Suite 700
San Francisco, CA 94102
(415) 864-5855

The Campaign for Women's
Health
666 11th St. NW, Suite 700
Washington, D.C. 20001
(202) 783-6686

Hispanic

Mexican American Legal Defense
Fund
634 South Spring St., 11th Floor
Los Angeles, CA 90014
(213) 629-2512

Movimiento Estudiantil Chicano de Aztlan
Box 4, Student Union Building
University of New Mexico
Albuquerque, NM 87131

National Council of La Raza
810 1st St. NE, #300
Washington, D.C. 20002
(202) 289-1380

Human Rights

American Civil Liberties Union
132 West 43rd St.
New York, NY 10036
(212) 944-9800, ext. 414

American-Arab
Anti-Discrimination Committee
4201 Connecticut Ave. NW
#500
Washington, D.C. 20036
(202) 244-2990

Amnesty International Youth Program
Amnesty International
1118 22nd St. NW
Washington, D.C. 20037
(202) 775-5161

Amnesty International
322 Eighth Ave.
New York, NY 10001
(212) 633-4200

Center for Third World Organizing
3861 Martin Luther King Jr. Way
Oakland, CA 94609
(510) 533-7583

Freedom Summer
c/o Andrew Goodman Foundation
350 West 31st St., 4th Floor South
New York, NY 10001
(212) 564-8694

Human Rights Resource Center
615 B St.
San Raphael, CA 94901
(415) 453-0404

Leadership Conference on Civil Rights
1629 K St. NW, #1010
Washington, D.C. 20006
(202) 466-3311

National Coalition Against Domestic Violence
P.O. Box 34103
Washington, D.C. 20043-4103
(202) 638-6388

Native American Rights Fund
1712 N St.
Washington, D.C. 20036
(202) 785-4166

Overseas Development Network
333 Valencia Street, #330
San Francisco, CA 94103
(415) 431-4204

Southern Poverty Law Center
400 Washington Ave.
Montgomery, AL 36104
(205) 264-0286

The Anti-Defamation League of
B'Nai B'Rith
823 United Nations Plaza
New York, NY 10017
(212) 490-2525

United National Indian Tribal
Youth (UNITY)
P.O. Box 25042
Oklahoma City, OK 73125
(405) 424-3010

Youth Works Center
1751 N St. NW, Suite 302
Washington, D.C. 20036
(202) 785-0764

Hunger/Homelessness

Bread for the World
1100 Wayne Ave., Suite 1000
Silver Springs, MD 20910
(301) 608-2400

Coalition for the Homeless
1234 Massachusetts Ave. NW
Washington, D.C. 20005
(202) 347-8870

Covenant House
460 West 41st St.
New York, NY 10036
(212) 613-0300

Empty the Shelters
1515 Fairmount Ave.
Philadelphia, PA 19130
(215) 765-4546

Habitat for Humanity
International
121 Habitat St.
Americus, GA 31709
(912) 924-6935
(800) HABITAT

National Alliance to End
Homelessness
1518 K St. NW, Suite 206
Washington, D.C. 20005
(202) 638-1526

National Coalition for the
Homeless
1612 K St. NW, Suite 1004
Washington, D.C. 20006
(202) 775-1322

National Low Income Housing
Coalition
1012 14th St. NW, Suite 1200
Washington, D.C. 20005
(202) 662-1530

National Neighborhood Coalition
810 1st St. NE
Washington, D.C. 20002
(202) 289-1551

National Student Campaign
Against Hunger and
Homelessness
29 Temple Pl.
Boston, MA 02111
(617) 292-4823

Oakland Potluck
Preservation Park
678 13th St.
Oakland, CA 94612
(510) 272-0414

Oxfam America
26 West St.
Boston, MA 02111
(617) 482-1211

Results
236 Massachusetts Ave. NE
Suite 300
Washington, D.C. 20002
(202) 543-9340

Second Harvest
116 South Michigan Ave., Suite 4
Chicago, IL 60603
(312) 263-2303

Youth Build
58 Day St.
P.O. Box 440322
Somerville, MA 02144
(617) 623-9900 ext. 1213

Politics/Action

Americans for Democratic Action
1625 K St. NW, Suite 210
Washington, D.C. 20006
(202) 785-5980

Citizen Action
1730 Rhode Island Ave. NW
Suite 403
Washington, D.C. 20036
(202) 775-1580

Citizens for Tax Justice
1311 L St. NW, Suite 400
Washington, D.C. 20005
(202) 626-3780

Common Cause
2030 M St. NW
Washington, D.C. 20036
(202) 833-1200

Congress Watch
215 Pennsylvania Ave. SE
Washington, D.C. 20003
(202) 546-4996

Democratic Leadership Council
518 C St. NE
Washington, D.C. 20002
(202) 546-0007

**Democratic National Committee
Youth Program**
430 S. Capitol St. SE
Washington, D.C. 20003
(202) 863-8183

Frontlash
815 16th St. NW
Washington, D.C. 20006
(202) 783-3993

Lead . . . or Leave
1606 20th St. NW
Washington, D.C. 20009
(202) 462-0808

National Abortion and
Reproductive Rights Action
League
1156 15th St. NW, #700
Washington, D.C. 20005
(202) 973-3000

National Teen Age Republican
Headquarters
P.O. Box 1896
Manassas, VA 22110
(703) 368-4214

Office of the President
1600 Pennsylvania Ave. NW
Washington, D.C. 20500
(202) 456-1414

Participation 2000
322 Massachusetts Ave. NE
Washington, D.C. 20002
(202) 543-5540

People for the American Way
2000 M St. NW, #400
Washington, D.C. 20036
(202) 467-4999

Public Citizen
2000 P St. NW
Washington, D.C. 20036
(202) 833-3000

Public Interest Research Groups
c/o NYPIRG
9 Murray St., 3rd Floor
New York, NY 10007-2272
(212) 349-6460

Southern Organizing
Committee–Youth Task Force
P.O. Box 10518
Atlanta, GA 30510
(404) 866-1987

USPIRG (United States Public
Interest Research Group)
215 Pennsylvania Ave. SE
Washington, D.C. 20003
(202) 546-9707

Vote America Foundation
1850 M St. NW, Suite 900
Washington, D.C. 20036
(202) 833-4210

Young Democrats of America
c/o Democratic National
Committee
430 S. Capitol St. SE
Washington, D.C. 20003
(202) 863-8000

Young Republican National
Federation
440 First St. NW, Suite 302
Washington, D.C. 20003
(202) 662-1340

Service

ACCESS: Networking in the
Public Interest/Community Jobs
Magazine
50 Beacon St.
Boston, MA 02108
(617) 720-5627

Break Away
6026 Station B
Nashville, TN 37235

Campus Compact
Box 1975
c/o Brown University
Providence, RI 02912
(401) 863-1119

**Campus Outreach Opportunity
League**
1101 15th St. NW, Suite 203
Washington, D.C. 20005
(202) 296-7017

Christmas in April USA
1225 Eye St. NW, Suite 601
Washington, D.C. 20005
(202) 326-8268

City Year
11 Stillings St., 2nd Floor
Boston, MA 02210
(617) 451-0699

CORO
95 Madison Ave., Suite 403
New York, NY 10016
(212) 683-8841

Corporation for National and
Community Service
1100 Vermont Ave. NW
Washington, D.C. 20525
(202) 606-5000

D.C. Service Corps
1511 K St. NW, Suite 949
Washington, D.C. 20005
(202) 347-4136

Do Something!
1 World Trade Center, 78th floor
New York, NY 10048
(212) 432-1110

Empowered Youth Educating
Society
c/o Encampment for Citizenship
2350 San Pablo Ave., Suite B
Berkeley, CA 94702-8908
(510) 548-8908

Everett Public Service Internship
635 Madison Ave., 8th Floor
New York, NY 10022

Literacy Volunteers of America
P.O. Box 73275
Washington, D.C. 20056
(202) 387-1772

National Association of Meal
Programs
101 N. Alfred St., Suite 202
Alexandria, VA 22314
(703) 548-5558

National Headquarters of the
YMCA
101 North Wacker, 14th Floor
Chicago, IL 60606
(312) 977-0031
(800) 872-9622

**National Youth Leadership
Council**
1910 W. County Road B
Room 214
Roseville, MN 55113
(612) 631-3672

Public Allies
1511 K St. NW, Suite 330
Washington, D.C. 20005
(202) 638-3300

Student Coalition for Action in Literacy Education (SCALE)
School of Education CB #3500
University of North Carolina,
Chapel Hill, NC 27599-3500
(919) 962-1542

Teach for America (TFA)
1 World Trade Center
78th Floor
New York, NY 10048
(800) 832-1230

Teens as Community Resources
100 Massachusetts Ave.
4th Floor
Boston, MA 02115
(617) 266-2788

The United Way National Headquarters
701 North Fairfax St.
Alexandria, VA 22314-2045
(703) 836-7100

VISTA Corporation of National Service
1100 Vermont Ave. NW
Washington, D.C. 20525
(202) 606-5000

Volunteer Centers/Points of Light Foundation
1737 H St. NW
Washington, D.C. 20006
(202) 223-9186

Young People for National Service
1730 Rhode Island Ave. NW
Washington, D.C. 20036

Youth Action
1830 Connecticut Ave. NW
Washington, D.C. 20009
(202) 483-1432

Youth Service America (YSA)
1101 15th St. NW, Suite 200
Washington, D.C. 20005
(202) 296-2992

Youth Works Center
1751 N St. NW, Suite 302
Washington, D.C. 20036
(202) 785-0764

Women

Center for Women Policy Studies
2000 P St. NW, Suite 508
Washington, D.C. 20036
(202) 872-1770

Fund for the Feminist Majority
1600 Wilson Blvd., Suite 801
Arlington, VA 22209
(703) 522-2214

League of Women Voters
1730 M St. NW, #1000
Washington, D.C. 20036
(202) 429-1965

National Organization for
Women
1000 16th St. NW, #700
Washington, D.C. 20036
(202) 331-0066

National Women's Law Center
1616 P St. NW, Suite 100
Washington, D.C. 20036
(202) 328-5160

National Women's Political
Caucus
1275 K St. NW, #750
Washington, D.C. 20005
(202) 898-1100

Republican Network to Elect
Women
1555 King St. NW, #200
P.O. Box 507
Alexandria, VA 22313
(703) 836-2255

Students Organizing Students
1600 Broadway, Suite 404
New York, NY 10019
(212) 977-6710

Third Wave
185 Franklin St., 3rd Floor
New York, NY 10013
(212) 925-3400

Wider Opportunities for Women
(WOW)
1325 G St. NW, Lower Level
Washington, D.C. 20005
(202) 638-3143

Women's Legal Defense Fund
1875 Connecticut Ave. NW
Suite 710
Washington, D.C. 20009
(202) 986-2600

Young Women's Project
1511 K St. NW, Suite 428
Washington, D.C. 20005
(202) 393-0461

CITIZEN ACTION GUIDES

Citizen Advocacy
Advocacy Institute
1730 Rhode Island Ave. NW
#600
Washington, D.C. 20036
(202) 659-8475

Citizen Action Guide
Bread for the World
802 Rhode Island Ave. NE
Washington, D.C. 20018
(301) 608-2400

Taxpayers Action Network
Citizens Against Government
Waste
1301 Connecticut Ave. NW
#400
Washington, D.C. 20036
(202) 467-5300

Strategic Media: Designing a
Public Education Campaign
Communications Consortium
1333 H St. NW, Suite 700
Washington, D.C. 20005
(202) 682-1270

Deficit Reduction Scorecard
The Concord Coalition
1025 Vermont Ave. NW, #810
Washington, D.C. 20005
(202) 737-1077

Congressional Voting Records
Consumer Federation of America
1424 16th St. NW, #604
Washington, D.C. 20036
(202) 387-6121

Community Action Kit
Greenpeace
1436 U St. NW, #305
Washington, D.C. 20009
(202) 462-1177

Getting Your Slice of Give Five
Independent Sector
1828 L St. NW, #1200
Washington, D.C. 20036
(202) 223-8100

National Environmental
Scorecard
Presidential Scorecard
League of Conservation Voters
1707 L St. NW, #550
Washington, D.C. 20036
(202) 785-8683

Publications Catalogue (extensive
citizen tools)
League of Women Voters
1730 M St. NW, #1000
Washington, D.C. 20036
(202) 429-1965

Rating of Congress
Taxpayer Action Guide
National Taxpayers' Union
325 Pennsylvania Ave. SE
Washington, D.C. 20003
(202) 543-1300

U.S. Congress Handbook
Anti-Censorship Kit
Organizing Kit
Phone Tree Packet
People for the American Way
2000 M St. NW, #400
Washington, D.C. 20036
(202) 467-4999

REGISTERING TO VOTE

Until the National Voter Registration Act of 1993 takes effect in 1995, registration requirements and procedures will vary widely from state to state. There are several ways to register new voters. States may currently utilize only one or some combination of these methods.

The easiest way to register is to fill out registration forms when you get your driver's license. You will often find registration tables on your campus or around your neighborhood near election times. Fill out the form at the site or mail it in when you get back home.

While there are some states in which you can register the day of the election (usually the first Tuesday of November in even years, like 1992, 1994, 1996), most require that you register a few weeks in advance, so plan ahead.

Voters may register at the polls in Maine, Minnesota, North Dakota, and Wisconsin. Voters in Alaska may register at the polls in presidential elections, and voters may register at the polls for the primaries in Wyoming.

For additional information, contact League of Women Voters state chapters or their national office at (202) 429-1965. To register to vote, you can directly contact the Office of the Secretary of State for your state and have the proper registration information sent to you.

State-by-State Numbers to Call for Voter Registration

State	Number	State	Number
Alabama	(205) 242-4337	Michigan	(517) 373-2540
Alaska	(907) 522-8683	Minnesota	(612) 296-9217
Arizona	(602) 542-8683	Mississippi	(601) 359-1350
Arkansas	(501) 682-6030	Missouri	(314) 751-2301
California	(800) 345-8683	Montana	(406) 444-2034
Colorado	(303) 894-2680	Nebraska	(402) 471-2554
Connecticut	(203) 566-3106	Nevada	(702) 687-5203
Delaware	(302) 739-4111	New Hampshire	(603) 271-3242
Florida	(904) 488-7690	New Jersey	(609) 292-3761
Georgia	(404) 656-2881	New Mexico	(505) 827-3620
Hawaii	(808) 586-0255	New York	(518) 474-6220
Idaho	(208) 334-2300	North Carolina	(919) 733-5140
Illinois	(217) 782-4141	North Dakota	(701) 224-2905
(Chicago)	(312) 814-6440	Ohio	(614) 466-2585
Indiana	(317) 232-6531	Oklahoma	(405) 521-3911
Iowa	(515) 281-5204	Oregon	(503) 378-4144
Kansas	(913) 296-2236	Pennsylvania	(717) 787-5280
Kentucky	(502) 573-2226	Rhode Island	(401) 277-2357
Louisiana	(504) 342-4479	South Carolina	(803) 734-9060
Maine	(207) 626-8400	South Dakota	(605) 773-3537
Maryland	(800) 232-8683	Tennessee	(615) 741-2819
Massachusetts	(617) 727-2828	Texas	(512) 463-5800

Utah	(801) 538-1040	Washington, D.C.	(202) 727-2525
Vermont	(802) 828-2363	West Virginia	(304) 558-6000
Virginia	(804) 786-2441	Wisconsin	(608) 266-5801
Washington	(206) 753-7121	Wyoming	(307) 777-5333

CONTACT YOUR NATIONAL LEADERS

Getting in touch with Washington only takes a few minutes, but once you've got your congressperson's phone, fax, address, and E-mail number, you can fire off any complaints and suggestions you want.

If you don't yet know who represents your interests in Washington, look in the front of any local phone book to find out. If you don't want to call the local office number listed, call (202) 224-3121 (that's the general operator for the United States Capital) and ask for the office of either your congressperson or your senators.

Once you contact the office, they'll usually take down your name and your concerns—and respond within a few weeks. The most effective letters and phone calls are targeted at an issue that's currently being debated in Congress. Be as specific as possible—staff often tally up calls for and against legislation and pass that on to the member.

What follows are the addresses and phone numbers for the White House, Congress, and a few of the main government agencies in Washington.

White House
1600 Pennsylvania Ave. NW
Washington, D.C. 20500
(202) 456-1414 (main switchboard)
(202) 456-2100 (Press Office)

Senate
Honorable [Your Member]
United States Senate
Washington, D.C. 20510
[his/her four-digit number]
(202) 224-3121

House of Representatives
Honorable [Your Member]
United States House of Representatives
Washington, D.C. 20515
[his/her four-digit number]
(202) 225-3121

Department of Education
400 Maryland Ave. SW
Washington, D.C. 20202
(202) 708-5366

Department of Energy
1000 Independence Ave. SW
Washington, D.C. 20585
(202) 586-5000

Department of Health and
Human Services
200 Independence Ave. SW
Washington, D.C. 20201
(202) 619-0257

Department of Housing and
Urban Development
451 7th St. SW
Washington, D.C. 20410
(202) 708-1112

Department of the Interior
18th and C Sts. NW
Washington, D.C. 20240
(202) 208-3100

Department of Justice
Constitution Ave. and
10th St. NW
Washington, D.C. 20530
(202) 514-2000

Department of Labor
200 Constitution Ave. NW
Washington, D.C. 20219
(202) 219-6666

Congressional Budget Office
Ford House Office Building
Room 405
Washington, D.C. 20515
(202) 226-2600

General Accounting Office
441 G St. NW
Washington, D.C. 20548
(202) 512-4800

United States Supreme Court
1 First St. NE
Washington, D.C. 20543
(202) 479-3000

CONTACT YOUR STATE LEADERS

Following is a list of the governors' offices by state, as well as the main
Washington office that represents all governors.

If you want more information on your current governor—such as
his/her voting record, number of years in office, stance on young people's
issues, etc.—simply contact the number listed below and take the same
steps that you would in contacting Congress.

National Governors' Association
444 North Capitol St. NW, #267
Washington, D.C. 20002
(202) 624-5300

Alabama
State Capitol
600 Dexter Ave.
Montgomery, AL 36130
(205) 242-7100

Alaska
P.O. Box 110001
Juneau, AK 99811-0001
(907) 465-3500

Arizona
State Capitol
1700 West Washington
Phoenix, AZ 85007
(602) 542-4331

Arkansas
State Capitol Bldg., Room 250
Little Rock, AR 72201
(501) 682-2345

California
State Capitol
Sacramento, CA 95814
(916) 445-2841

Colorado
136 State Capitol
Denver, CO 80203-1792
(303) 866-2471

Connecticut
210 Capitol Ave.
Hartford, CT 06106
(203) 566-4840

Delaware
Legislative Hall
Dover, DE 19901
(302) 739-4101

Florida
The Capitol
Tallahassee, FL 32399
(904) 488-2272

Georgia
203 State Capitol
Atlanta, GA 30334
(404) 656-1776

Hawaii
State Capitol
235 South Beretania
Honolulu, HI 96813
(808) 586-0034

Idaho
State House
Boise, ID 83720-1000
(208) 334-2100

Illinois
State Capitol, Room 207
Springfield, IL 63706
(217) 782-6830

Indiana
State House, Room 206
Indianapolis, IN 46204
(317) 232-4567

Iowa
State Capitol Building
Des Moines, IA 50319-0001
(515) 281-5211

Kansas
State House, 2nd Floor
Topeka, KS 66612-1590
(913) 296-3232

Kentucky
State Capitol
700 Capitol St.
Frankfort, KY 40801
(502) 564-2611

Louisiana
P.O. Box 94004
Baton Rouge, LA 70804-9004
(504) 342-7015

Maine
State House
Station 1
Augusta, ME 04333
(207) 289-3531

Maryland
State House
Annapolis, MD 21401
(410) 974-3901

Massachusetts
State House, Room 360
Boston, MA 02133
(617) 727-9173

Michigan
P.O. Box 30013
Lansing, MI 48909
(517) 373-3400

Minnesota
75 Constitution Ave.
130 State Capitol
St. Paul, MN 55155
(612) 296-3391

Mississippi
P.O. Box 139
Jackson, MS 39205
(601) 359-3100

Missouri
P.O. Box 720
Jefferson City, MO 65102
(314) 751-3222

Montana
Capitol Station
Helena, MT 59620-0801
(406) 444-3111

Nebraska
P.O. Box 94848
Lincoln, NE 68509-4848
(402) 471-2244

Nevada
State Capitol
Carson City, NV 89710
(702) 687-5670

New Hampshire
Office of the Governor
Room 208
Concord, NH 03301
(603) 271-2121

New Jersey
125 West State St.
CN-001
Trenton, NJ 08625
(609) 292-6000

New Mexico
State Capitol, 4th Floor
Santa Fe, NM 87503
(505) 827-3000

New York
State Capitol
Albany, NY 12224
(518) 474-8390

North Carolina
State Capitol
Capitol Square
Raleigh, NC 27603
(919) 733-4240

North Dakota
600 East Boulevard Ave.
Bismarck, ND 58505
(701) 224-2200

Ohio
77 South High St., 30th Floor
Columbus, OH 43266-0601
(614) 466-3355

Oklahoma
State Capitol Building
Suite 212
Oklahoma City, OK 73105
(405) 521-2342

Oregon
254 State Capitol
Salem, OR 97310
(503) 378-3100

Pennsylvania
Main Capitol Building
Room 225
Harrisburg, PA 17120
(717) 787-2500

Rhode Island
State House
Providence, RI 03903
(401) 277-2080

South Carolina
P.O. Box 11969
Columbia, SC 29211
(803) 734-9818

South Dakota
500 East Capitol
Pierre, SD 57501
(605) 773-3212

Tennessee
State Capitol
Nashville, TN 37243-0001
(615) 741-2001

Texas
P.O. Box 12428
Austin, TX 78711
(512) 463-2000

Utah
210 State Capitol
Salt Lake City, UT 84114
(801) 538-1000

Vermont
Pavillion Office Building
100 State St.
Montpelier, VT 05609
(802) 828-3333

Virginia
State Capitol
Richmond, VA 23219
(804) 786-2211

Washington
Legislative Building
Olympia, WA 98504-0002
(206) 753-6780

West Virginia
State Capitol Complex
Charleston, WV 25305-0370
(304) 338-3000

Wisconsin
State Capitol
P.O. Box 7863
Madison, WI 53707
(608) 266-1212

Wyoming
State Capitol
Cheyenne, WY 82002
(307) 777-7434

MAINSTREAM NEWSPAPERS AND MAGAZINES

Another easy way to get involved is writing letters to the editor of either
your local paper or any of the top national and regional media we've
listed here. You might even write your own editorial. To find out the name
of your hometown paper's editor, look at the front page or inside page of
the paper and the staff will be listed.

Boston Globe
(617) 929-2000

Letters to the Editor; Editorials
The Boston Globe
P.O. Box 2378
Boston, MA 02107-2378

Business Week
(212) 512-2511

Letters to the Editor; Editorials
Business Week
1221 Avenue of the Americas
39th Floor
New York, NY 10020

Chicago Tribune
(312) 222-3232

Letters to the Editor; Editorials
Chicago Tribune
435 North Michigan Ave.
Chicago, IL 60611

Dallas Morning News
(800) 431-0010

Letters to the Editor; Editorials
Rena Peterson
Dallas Morning News
Communications Center
P.O. Box 655237
Dallas, TX 75265

Detroit Free Press
(313) 222-6400

Letters to the Editor; Editorials
Detroit Free Press
321 West Lafayette Blvd.
Detroit, MI 48226

Fortune
(212) 522-1212

Letters to the Editor; Editorials
Fortune Magazine
Time & Life Building
Rockefeller Center
New York, NY 10020

Hartford Courant
(203) 241-6200

Letters to the Editor; Editorials
Hartford Courant
285 Broad St.
Hartford, CT 06115

Kansas City Star
(816) 234-4141

Letters to the Editor; Editorials
Kansas City Star
1729 Grand Avenue
Kansas City, MO 64108

Los Angeles Times
(213) 237-5000

Letters to the Editor; Editorials
Times Mirror Square
Los Angeles, CA 90053

The Nation
(212) 242-8400

Letters to the Editor; Editorials
The Nation
72 5th Ave.
New York, NY 10011

The New Republic
(202) 331-7494

Letters to the Editor; Editorials
The New Republic
1220 19th St. NW
Suite 600
Washington, D.C. 20036

New York Times
(212) 556-1234
Fax: (212) 556-3690

Letters to the Editor; Editorials
The New York Times
229 West 43rd St.
New York, NY 10036

Newsday
(516) 843-2020

Letters to the Editor; Editorials
Newsday
235 Pinelawn
Melville, NY 11744

Newsweek
(800) 631-1040
Fax: (212) 350-4120
Telephone Mail Desk:
(900) 990-MAIL

Letters Editor, Newsweek
444 Madison Avenue
New York, NY 10022

Letters for "My Turn":
Ms. Olwen Clarke
Newsweek
444 Madison Avenue
New York, NY 10022
(212) 350-4000

The Orlando Sentinel
(407) 420-5000

Letters to the Editor; Editorials
The Orlando Sentinel
633 North Orange
Orlando, FL 32801-1349

Philadelphia Inquirer
(215) 854-2000

Letters to the Editor; Editorials
Philadelphia Inquirer
P.O. Box 8263
Philadelphia, PA 19101

San Francisco Examiner
(415) 777-2424

Letters to the Editor; Editorials
San Francisco Examiner
110 5th St.
San Francisco, CA 94103

Time
(212) 522-1212
Fax: (212) 522-0601

Time Magazine Letters
Time & Life Building
Rockefeller Center
New York, NY 10020

USA Today
(800) USA-0001
(800) 828-0909

USA Today
Letters to the Editor; Editorials
1000 Wilson Blvd.
Arlington, VA 22229

U.S. News & World Report
(202) 955-2000

Letters to the Editor
U.S. News & World Report
2400 N St. NW
Washington, D.C. 20037

The Wall Street Journal
(212) 416-2000
Fax: (212) 416-2658

Letters to the Editor; Editorials
The Wall Street Journal
200 Liberty Street
New York, NY 10281

The Washington Post
(202) 334-6000

Letters to the Editor; Editorials
The Washington Post
1150 15th St. NW
Washington, D.C. 20071

The Washington Times
(202) 636-3000

Letters to the Editor
The Washington Times
3600 New York Ave. NE
Washington, D.C. 20002

Editorials
Mary Lou Forbes
Commentary Editor
The Washington Times
3600 New York Ave. NE
Washington, D.C. 20002

II: ALTERNATIVE MEDIA

The 1990s may be remembered as the decade when "alternative" media took over, from call-in talk shows that have the power to block a congressional pay raise to the new technologies that are changing the way we communicate. Whether it's in the form of a fanzine, cable access television, pirate radio, Internet discussion forums, on-line bulletin boards, or even glossy magazines, new voices are getting heard and they're often from our generation.

The following resource guide highlights some of the latest and greatest new media outlets, as well as a few alternative press sources that have been around for a while. The list is by no means comprehensive, since many new magazines, cable-access shows, and radio programs are only available locally. And the rising popularity of 'zines on various topics makes it impossible to list them—check out *The World of Zines*, a book by Mike Gunderloy and Cari Goldberg Janice, for an overview of the most promising entries.

Finally, on-line networks and bulletin boards are another great source of information and ideas. For the uninitiated, it may be difficult to become familiar with the vagaries of modems, communication programs, and on-line access. But it's definitely worth the effort.

Services like CompuServe, America On-Line, GEnie, and Prodigy offer customized information packages, and many companies offer full access to the Internet. Either way, you will be able to exchange electronic mail quickly and easily with almost anybody in the world.

GENERATION X MAGAZINES

Following is a list of some of the best Generation X magazines. While they vary in circulation, all are young and could use your support as a subscriber (and maybe even as a contributor).

AdBusters
The Media Foundation
1243 West 7th Ave.
Vancouver, B.C. Canada
V6H 1B7
(604) 736-9401
adbuster @ wimsey.com

and . . .
P.O. Box 5905448
San Francisco, CA
94159-0548

Axcess
P.O. Box 9309
San Diego, CA 92169
(800) 4AXCESS
editor @ axcess.com

Bikini
2110 Main St., Suite 100
Santa Monica, CA 90405
(310) 452-6222
bikini @ mcimail.com

Buzzworm:
The Environmental Journal
2305 Canyon Blvd., Suite 206
Boulder, CO 80302

Details
632 Broadway, 12th Floor
New York, NY 10012
(212) 420-0689
detailsmag @ aol.com

Diversity and Division
Madison Center for
Education Affairs
P.O. Box 472
White Plains, MD 20695-9700
(202) 833-1801

E: The Environmental Magazine
Earth Action Network, Inc.
P.O. Box 5098
Westport, CT 06881
(203) 854-5559

Envision Magazine
4950 William Penn Hwy.
Export, PA 15632
(415) 327-2327

Exec
Rodale Press
33 East Minor St.
Emmaus, PA 18098
(215) 967-5171

Fast Company
1100 Massachusetts Ave.
Cambridge, MA 02138
(617) 497-1361
fastcompany @ mcimail.com

Garbage
2 Main St.
Gloucester, MA 01930
(508) 283-3200

h2504
P.O. Box 423354
San Francisco, CA 94142

Hum
544 2nd St.
San Francisco, CA 94107

Hypno
624 Broadway, 3rd Floor
San Diego, CA 92101
(619) 696-9852

Inside Edge
P.O. Box 712
Cambridge, MA 02238
(617) 497-5621

Insider
4214 Oakton St.
Skokie, IL 60076-3267

io: Literary Culture
P.O. Box 164254
Austin, TX 78716
(512) 469-7447

Karma Lapel
P.O. Box 5467
Evanston, IL 60204-5467

KGB Magazine
133 The Bowery
New York, NY 10002
(212) 343-1512
kgbmag @ aol.com

Link
188 Sherwood Place
Englewood, NJ 07631
(201) 816-8777

Lumpen Times
2558 West Armitage
Chicago, IL 60647
(312) 227-2072

Might
544 2nd St.
San Francisco, CA 94107
(415) 896-1528
Fax: (415) 896-1512
mightmag @ aol.com

Mondo 2000
P.O. Box 10171
Berkeley, CA 94709-0171

The Next Progressive
P.O. Box 18713
Washington, D.C. 20036
(202) 828-3059

The Nose
P.O. Box 31353
San Francisco, CA 94131
(415) 541-9856
jacknose @ well.com

OUT Magazine
110 Greene St., Suite 600
New York, NY 10012-3812
(212) 334-9119

Page One
Monticello Publishing
118 W. Streetsboro Rd.
Suite 129
Hudson, OH 44236
(216) 655-9856
Fax: (216) 650-6781

Paper
529 Broadway
New York, NY 10012
(212) 226-4405
papermag @ aol.com

Project X
37 West 20th St., Suite 1007
New York, NY 10011
(212) 366-6603

Pure
P.O. Box 25665
Chicago, IL 60625
(312) 772-5570

RayGun
1223 Wilshire Blvd., Suite 819
Santa Monica, CA 90403

Soma
285 9th St.
San Francisco, CA 94103
(415) 558-8974

Student Travels
376 Boylston St.
Boston, MA 02116
(617) 424-7700

The Third Word
25 East Delaware, Suite 205
Chicago, IL 60611
(312) 642-0288
thirdworld @ aol.com

U (The National College
Magazine)
1800 Century Park East
Suite 820
Los Angeles, CA 90067
(310) 551-1381
Fax: (310) 551-1659

Utne Reader
1624 Harmon Place,
Suite 330
Minneapolis, MN 55403
(800) 736-UTNE

Who Cares
1511 K St. NW, Suite 1042
Washington, D.C. 20005
(202) 628-1691
whocares @ cec.org

Wired
544 2nd St.
San Francisco, CA
94107-1427
(415) 904-0660
info @ wired.com

Z Magazine
18 Millfield St.
Woods Hole, MA 02543
(508) 548-9063

THE INTERNET

The Internet allows people across the globe to exchange ideas and information. Consisting of a "web" of computers, the "net" allows instantaneous communication and information transfer. As Lead . . . or Leave and other advocacy organizations have discovered, the Internet is the logical next wave for political organizing.

Getting On

There are two requirements: a computer with a modem, and an Internet access point.

If you're a new user, getting connected is the hardest part. You need a service provider that will allow you to plug your computer into the Internet via their connection point. You might have this access through your school or workplace. Check that out first.

- If you're a student, this means calling the school's central computer facility or academic adviser.
- In the workplace, talk to the systems administrator of your company's local network.
- As a last resort, if there is no connection available, write up a proposal to get the office or university connected.

Several cities have "freenets"—local Internet connections for public use. If there is a freenet near you, there may be open terminals in the local public library.

If you continue to have trouble gaining access, do a little detective work. While in the library check out some of these books:

- *Free Electronic Networks* by William J. Shefski
- *The Internet Guide for New Users* by Daniel P. Dern
- *The Whole Internet User's Guide and Catalog* by Ed Krol

There are numerous other books about the Internet, but these three offer a good starting point. They will prove invaluable for finding the connection, and learning about navigating the world of computers.

Internet Resources

There is a massive amount of information available to an experienced user. The following is a short list of helpful Internet resources:

Government Fax and Phone Numbers:
    ftp wuarchive.wustl.edu; login anonymous; cd doc/policy
                                                    /academic
                                                    /civics
    ftp pit-manager.mit.edu; login anonymous; cd pub/activism
                                                    /congress

Government Programs and Information:
    WAIS US-gov-programs.sr
    telnet fedix.fie.com;login bbs
    ftp wiretap.spies.com; login anonymous; cd pub/Clinton
                                                    /Economic Plan
                                                    /GAO_Reports
                                                    /Gov/US Docs
                                                    /US-Gov
                                                    /US-State

Sources:
Krol, Ed. *The Whole Internet*. Sebastopol, Calif.: O'Reilly and Associates, 1993.
Tolhurst, William A., et al. *Using the Internet*. Indianapolis, Ind.: Que Corporation, 1994.

TOP RADIO TALK SHOWS

Don't be bashful about using this list. Read the newspaper in the morning, tune in to any of these shows during the day, and don't hesitate to call in. Far too often the only callers are older listeners—and most of these shows are eager to let younger callers get through.

Here is a list of more than three dozen of the most listened-to radio shows as provided by the National Association of Radio Talk Show Hosts.

Rush Limbaugh, Host
Kit Carson, Producer
"Rush Limbaugh Show"
WABC-AM
2 Penn Plaza, 17th Floor
New York, NY 10121
Tel: (212) 613-3800
Fax: (212) 563-9166

Larry King, Host
Patrick Piper, Producer
"Larry King"
Mutual Broadcasting System
1755 South Jefferson Davis
Highway
Arlington, VA 22202
Tel: (703) 413-8375
Fax: (703) 413-8444

Paul Harvey, Host
June Westguard, Contact
"Paul Harvey News"
ABC Radio Network
333 North Michigan Ave.
Suite 1600
Chicago, IL 60601
Tel: (312) 899-4085
Fax: (312) 899-4088

Gene Burns, Host
Larry Kahn, Producer
"Gene Burns"
WOR-AM Radio
1440 Broadway
New York, NY 10022
Tel: (212) 642-4558
Fax: (212) 642-4486

Jim Bohannon, Host
Patrick Piper, Producer
"Jim Bohannon Show"
Mutual Broadcasting System
1755 South Jefferson Davis
Highway
Arlington, VA 22202
Tel: (703) 413-8375
Fax: (703) 413-8444

Mike Siegel, Host
"Mike Siegel Show"
KVI Radio and Chancellor
Broadcasting Company
200 Tower Building
Seattle, WA 98101
Tel: (206) 223-5700
Fax: (206) 292-1015

Michael Reagan, Host
David Berg, Producer
"Michael Reagan Show"
c/o American Entertainment
Network
P.O. Box 1548
La Jolla, CA 92038
Tel: (800) 345-3113
Fax: (619) 754-3344

Doug Stephan, Host
"Good Day, USA" (Syndicated)
1084 Grove St.
Framingham, MA 01701
Tel: (508) 877-8700
Fax: (508) 877-8860

Mary Beal, Host
Independent Broadcasters
Network & KNSS
2402 East 37th St.
Wichita, KS 67219
Tel: (316) 832-9600
Fax: (316) 832-9688

Jack Anderson, Host
Ed Henry, Producer
"National Forum"
Independent Broadcasters
Network
1200 Eton Ct. NW, Suite 300
Washington, D.C. 20007
Tel: (202) 944-3030
Fax: (202) 944-3359

Michael Jackson, Host
Ted Lekas, Producer
"Michael Jackson Show"
KABC-AM
3321 South La Cienega Blvd.
Los Angeles, CA 90016
Tel: (310) 840-4901
Fax: (310) 837-1955
Mr. Jackson prefers not to have
information faxed.

Shows hosted by Alan Colmes;
Morton Downey, Jr.; Barry
Farber; Lee Mirabal; and Leslie
Marshall
Julia Heath, Senior Producer
Major Talk (Radio Network)
125 West End Ave., 6th Floor
New York, NY 10023
Tel: (212) 456-5595
Fax: (212) 877-1413

Bruce Williams, Host
Bruce Williams, Producer
"Bruce Williams Show"
NBC Talknet/Westwood
8038 State Road, #54
New Port Richey, FL 34653
Tel: (813) 376-4111

Howard Stern, Host
Gary Dell'Apate, Producer
"Howard Stern Show"
(Syndicated)
WXRK-FM
600 Madison Ave.
New York, NY 10022
Tel: (212) 750-0550
Fax: (212) 832-9544

Michael S. Harrison, Host
"Countdown"
c/o Talkers
95 Oakwood Dr.
Longmeadow, MA 01106
Tel: (413) 567-3189

Don Imus, Host
Bernard McGuirk, Producer
"Imus in the Morning"
(Syndicated)
WFAN-AM
3412 36th St.
Astoria, NY 11106
Tel: (718) 706-7650
Fax: (718) 706-6481

Ronn Owens, Host
Mikel Cleland, Producer
"Ronn Owens Show"
KBO-AM
900 Front St.
San Francisco, CA 94111
Tel: (415) 954-8140
Fax: (415) 362-5827

Chuck Baker, Host
Rinda Butler, Producer
"Chuck Baker Show"
KVOR-AM / KSPZ-FM
2864 South Circle Dr.
Suite 150
Colorado Springs, CO 80906
Tel: (719) 540-9200
Fax: (719) 579-0882

Mike Rosen, Host
David Lawrence, Producer
"Mike Rosen Show"
KOA-AM
1380 Lawrence St., Suite 1300
Denver, CO 80204
Tel: (303) 893-8500
Fax: (303) 892-4700

Ken Hamblin
"Ken Hamblin Show"
KNUS-AM
5800 West Alameda Avenue
Lakewood, CO 80226
Tel: (303) 935-7171
Fax: (303) 935-0954

Carlotta Bradley, Host
(Afternoon Drive)
"Carlotta Bradley Show"
WDEL-AM
2727 Shipley Rd.
P.O. Box 7492
Wilmington, DE 19803
Tel: (302) 478-2700
Fax: (302) 478-0100

Mark Williams, Host
"Mark Williams Show"
WFLA Radio
4002 Gandy Blvd.
Tampa, FL 33611
Tel: (813) 839-9393
Fax: (813) 278-0423

Mark Scheinbaum, Host
"Mark Scheinbaum Show"
Jack Cole, Host
"Jack Cole Show"
WJNO-AM
433 Plaza Real
Suite 355
Boca Raton, FL 33432
Tel: (800) 677-1107
Fax: (407) 838-4357

Studs Terkel, Host
Lois Baum, Producer
"Studs Terkel Show"
WFMT-FM
303 East Wacker Dr.
Chicago, IL 60601
Tel: (312) 565-5000
Fax: (312) 565-5169

Jonathan Brandmeir
Host/Producer
"Jonathan Brandmeir Show"
WLUP-AM
875 North Michigan Ave.
Suite 3750
Chicago, IL 60611
Tel: (312) 440-5270
Fax: (312) 440-9896

Bob Collins, Host
Laurel Homer, Producer
"Bob Collins Show"
WGN-AM
435 North Michigan Avenue
Chicago, IL 60611
Tel: (312) 222-4700
Fax: (312) 222-5165

David Brudnoy, Host
John McLaine and Lauren
Brown, Producers
Kevin Myron, Bookings
"David Brudnoy Show"
WBZ-AM
1170 Soldiers Field Rd.
Boston, MA 02134
Tel: (617) 787-7241
Fax: (617) 787-7392

Shows hosted by Marjorie
Clapprood and (Mr.) Pat Whitley;
Steven J. J. Weisman; Jerry
Williams; and Eileen Prose
Paula O'Connor, Executive
Producer
WRKO-AM
3 Fenway Plaza
116 Huntington Ave.
Boston, MA 02116
Tel: (617) 236-6800
Fax: (617) 236-6834

J. P. McCarthy, Host
Mike Shiels, Producer
"J. P. McCarthy Morning Show"
WJR-AM
2100 Fisher Building
Detroit, MI 48202
Tel: (313) 875-4440
Fax: (313) 875-9022

Charles Brennan, Host
"Charles Brennan Show"
KMOX-AM (CBS)
One Memorial Dr.
St. Louis, MO 63102
Tel: (314) 444-3278
Fax: (314) 444-3230

Bob Grant, Host
Bob Bucci, Executive Producer
"Bob Grant Show"
WABC-AM
2 Penn Plaza, 17th Floor
New York, NY 10121
Tel: (212) 613-3839
Fax: (212) 947-1340

Ed Shultz, Jeanette Stanton, the
Kirschners, and Boyd
Christenson, Hosts/Producers
"Viewpoint"
WDAY-AM
301 South 8th St.
Fargo, ND 58108
Tel: (701) 241-5350
Fax: (701) 241-5373

Mike Pintek, Host
Greg Jena, Executive Producer
"Mike Pintek Show"
KDKA-AM
One Gateway Center
Pittsburgh, PA 15222
Tel: (412) 575-2200
Fax: (412) 575-2873

Les Jameson, Host
Patrick Hennessy, Producer
"Les Jameson Show"
WLAC-AM
10 Music Circle East
Nashville, TN 37203
Tel: (615) 256-0555
Fax: (615) 242-4826

David Gold, Host
(Ms.) Pepi Harris, Producer
"David Gold Show"
KLIF-AM
3500 Maple Ave., Suite 1600
Dallas, TX 75219
Tel: (214) 526-2400
Fax: (214) 520-4343

Carl Wigglesworth, Host
Lori Wigglesworth, Producer
"Wigglesworth Show"
WOAI-AM
6222 Northwest I-10
San Antonio, TX 78201
Tel: (210) 736-9700
Fax: (510) 735-8811

G. Gordon Liddy, Host
"G. Gordon Liddy Show"
WJFK
10800 Main St.
Fairfax, VA 22030
Tel: (703) 691-1900

Bradley S. O'Leary, Co-Host
"O'Leary Kamber Radio Report"
3050 K St. NW, Suite 105
Washington, D.C. 20036
Tel: (202) 944-4550
Fax: (202) 944-4560

III: SOURCES AND SUGGESTED READING

Chapter One

Barone, Michael. *The Almanac of American Politics: 1994.* Edited by Grant Ujifusa. New York: Macmillan, 1994.

Cohn, Jonathon S. "A Lost Political Generation." *The American Prospect.*

Dey, Eric L., Alexander W. Astin, Willian S. Korn, and Ellyne R. Riggs. *The American Freshman: National Norms for Fall, 1992.* Los Angeles: U.C.L.A. Higher Education Research Institute, 1992.

Dunn, William. *The Baby Bust: A Generation Comes of Age.* Chicago: American Demographic Books, 1993.

Ginsberg, Benjamin, and Martin Shefter. *Politics by Other Means: The Declining Importance of Elections in America.* New York: Basic Books, 1991.

Gross, David M., and Sophrfonnia Scott. "Proceeding with Caution." *Time,* July 16, 1990.

Howe, Neil, and William Strauss. "The New Generation Gap." *The Atlantic Monthly,* December 1992.

Kettering Foundation. *Citizens and Politics: A View from Main Street.* The Kettering Foundation, 1991.

People for the American Way. *Democracy's Next Generation.* Washington, D.C.: The People for the American Way, 1989.

Phillips, Kevin P. *The Politics of Rich and Poor.* New York: Random House, Inc., 1990.

Population Reference Bureau Inc. "Twentysomething Group Evades Easy Labels." *Population Today,* Volume 20 (November 1992).

Ratan, Suneel. "How to Really Cut the Budget Deficit." *Fortune*, October 4, 1993.

Strauss, William, and Neil Howe. *Generations: The History of America's Future: 1584 to 2069.* New York: William Morrow and Company, 1991.

Strauss, William, Neil Howe, and Ian Williams. *Thirteenth Generation: Abort, Retry, Ignore, Fail?* New York: Vintage Books, 1993.

Chapter Two

Attarian, John. "Facing the Deficit, No Time for Gimmicks." *National Review*.

Barlett, Donald L., and James B. Steele. *America: What Went Wrong.* Kansas City, Mo.: Andrews and McMeel, 1992.

Besharov, Douglas J. "Budget Myths: Six Myths about the Reagan/Bush Budgets (and a Lesson for Bill Clinton)." *The American Enterprise*, September/October 1993.

Black, Eric. "Everything You Always Wanted to Know about the Debt and a Whole Lot More." *The Minneapolis Star Tribune*, August 22, 1993.

Brockenbrough, Martha. "National Debt, Social Security and the New Generational Warfare." *Envision*, 1993.

Clinton, Bill. *The Economic Report of the President.* Washington, D.C.: GPO, 1994.

Concord Coalition. *The Zero Deficit Plan: A Plan for Eliminating the Federal Budget Deficit by the Year 2000.* Washington, D.C.: The Concord Coalition, 1993.

Congressional Budget Office. *Assessing the Decline in the National Savings Rate.* Washington, D.C.: GPO, 1993.

———. *Baby Boomers in Retirement: An Early Perspective.* Washington, D.C.: GPO, 1993.

———. *The Economic and Budget Outlook: Fiscal Years 1994–1998.* Washington, D.C.: GPO, 1993.

———. *The Economic and Budget Update.* Washington, D.C.: GPO, 1993.

———. *Federal Debt and Interest Costs.* Washington, D.C.: GPO, 1993.

———. *Reducing the Size of the Federal Civilian Work Force.* Washington, D.C.: GPO, 1993.

———. *Trends in Health Spending, An Update.* Washington, D.C.: GPO, 1993.

Congressional Quarterly Incorporated Staff, Special Report. *Where the Money Goes: A Comprehensive Guide to the 1994 Spending Choices of Clinton and Congress.* Washington, D.C.: Congressional Quarterly, Special Report, 1993.

Council for Citizens against Government Waste. *A Revolution in Government: Critical Government Waste Issues for the Clinton Administration and the 103rd Congress.* Washington, D.C.: Council for Citizens against Government Waste, 1993.

Council on Competitiveness. *Competitiveness Index.* Washington, D.C.: The Council on Competitiveness, 1993.

"Debt Spree Leaves a Painful Legacy." *The Washington Post,* September 27, 1992.

Dentzer, Susan. "America's Investment Crisis." *U.S. News and World Report,* February 24, 1992.

Eisner, Robert. "Sense and Nonsense about Budget Deficits." *Harvard Business Review,* 1993.

Figgie, Harry. *Bankruptcy 1995: The Coming Collapse of America and How to Stop It.* Boston: Little, Brown and Company, 1992.

Garland, Susan B. "A Way out of the Morass." *Business Week,* October 23, 1992.

General Accounting Office. *The Budget Deficit: Outlook, Implications and Choices.* Washington, D.C.: GPO, 1990.

———. *Budget Policy: Long-term Implications of the Deficit, Statement of Charles A. Bowsher, Comptroller General of the United States.* Washington, D.C.: GPO, 1992.

———. *Budget Policy: Prompt Action Necessary to Avert Long-term Damage to the Economy.* Washington, D.C.: GPO, 1993.

———. *The Economic and Budget Outlook: Fiscal Years 1994–1998.* Washington, D.C.: GPO, 1993.

"The Green Solution to Red Ink: Cutting Wasteful and Environmentally Harmful Subsidies and Spending—The Clinton Plan and Additional Cuts." *Friends of the Earth,* March 23, 1993.

Hershey, Robert D. "Why Economists Fear the Deficit." *The New York Times,* May 5, 1992.

Jost, Kenneth et al. "Downward Mobility: What Happened to the American Dream?" *CQ Researcher,* July 23, 1993.

Kettl, Donald F. *Deficit Politics: Public Budgeting in Its Institutional and Historical Context.* New York: Macmillan Publishing Company, 1991.

Longman, Phillip. *Generational Equity in an Aging Society.* The Center for Public Policy and Contemporary Issues, 1991.

Malabre, Alfred L., Jr. *Beyond Our Means.* New York: Random House, Inc., 1987.

Mishel, Lawrence, and Jared Bernstein. *The Joyless Recovery: Deteriorating Wages and Job Quality in the 1980s.* Washington, D.C.: Economic Policy Institute, 1993.

———. *The State of Working America: 1992–1993.* Armonk, N.Y.: M. E. Sharpe, Inc., 1993.

Moore, Stephen. "Government: America's #1 Growth Industry." *Institute for Policy Innovation,* February 1993.

National Issues Forum Institute Staff. *The $4 Trillion Debt: Tough Choices about Soaring Federal Deficits.* Dubuque, Ia.: Kendall/Hunt Publishing, Inc., 1994.

Newman, Katherine S. *Declining Fortunes: The Withering of the American Dream.* New York: Basic Books, 1993.

Nunn, Sam, Pete Domenici, and Debra L. Miller. *The CSIS Strengthening of America Commission, First Report.* Westport, Conn.: Center for Strategic and International Studies, 1992.

O'Reilly, Brian. "The Job Drought." *Fortune,* July 24, 1992.

Perot, Ross. *Not for Sale at Any Price: How We Can Save America for Our Children.* New York: Hyperion, 1993.

———. *United We Stand: How We Can take Back Our Country.* New York: Hyperion, 1992.

Peterson, Peter G. *Facing Up: How to Rescue the Economy from Crushing Debt and Restore the American Dream.* New York: Simon and Schuster, Inc., 1993.

Phillips, Kevin. *Boiling Point: Democrats, Republicans, and the Decline of Middle Class Prosperity.* New York: Random House, Inc., 1993.

———. *The Politics of Rich and Poor: Wealth and the American Electorate in the Reagan Aftermath.* New York: HarperCollins Publishers, 1991.

Supplement to the President's Budget. Washington, D.C.: Historical Tables, 1993.

Tsongas, Paul E. *A Call to Economic Arms: Forging a New American Mandate.* The Tsongas Committee, 1991.

U.S. Congress Committee for Economic Development. *Fighting Federal Deficits: The Time for Hard Choices.* Washington, D.C.: GPO, 1984.

U.S. Government. *Budget of the U.S. Government, Fiscal Year 1993.* Washington, D.C.: GPO, 1993.

U.S. House Committee on Ways and Means. *1993 Greenbook, Overview of Entitlement Programs.* Washington, D.C.: GPO, 1993.

Van Doorn, Ooms. "Budget Priorities of the Nation." *Science*, December 11, 1992.

Chapter Three

Aschauer, David. *Public Investment and Private Sector Growth: The Economic Benefits of Reducing America's "Third Deficit."* Washington, D.C.: Economic Policy Institute, 1990.

Bennett, William J. *American Education: Making It Work.* Washington, D.C.: U.S. Department of Education, 1988.

Black Community Crusade for Children Staff. *Progress and Peril: Black Children in America.* Washington, D.C.: The Children's Defense Fund, 1991.

Bread for the World. *Hunger 1994: Transferring the Politics of Hunger.* Washington, D.C.: Bread for the World Institute, 1994.

"The Brokaw Report: The Lost Generation." National Broadcasting Company, Inc., 1993.

Buderi, Robert, and Joseph Weber. "On a Clear Day, You Can See Progress." *Business Week*, June 29, 1992.

Center for the Study of Social Policy. *1993 Kids Count Data Book: State Profiles of Child Well-being.* Washington, D.C.: Center for the Study of Social Policy, 1993.

Children's Defense Fund Staff. *The State of the Children: 1992.* Washington, D.C.: The Children's Defense Fund, 1992.

———. *Decade of Indifference: Maternal and Child Health Trends, 1980–1990.* Washington, D.C.: The Children's Defense Fund, 1993.

Committee for Economic Development. *Investing in Our Children.* New York: Committee for Economic Development, 1985.

Families First: Report of the National Commission on America's Urban Families. Upland, Penn.: Diane Publishing Company, 1993.

Gerald, Debra E., and William J. Hussar. *Projections of Education Statistics to 2003.* Washington, D.C.: GPO, 1992.

Gest, Ted, Gordon Witkin, Katia Hetter, and Andrea Wright. "Violence in America." *U.S. News and World Report*, January 17, 1994.

Grant, James P. *The State of the World's Children, 1993.* New York: Oxford University Press, 1993.

Hewlett, Sylvia Ann. *When the Bough Breaks: The Cost of Neglecting Our Children.* New York: Basic Books, 1991.

Hoffman, Charlene M. *Federal Support for Education, Fiscal Years 1980 to 1981*. Washington, D.C.: GPO, 1991.

Johnston, Lloyd D., Ph.D., Patrick O'Malley, Ph.D., and Jerald Bachman, Ph.D. *Smoking, Drinking and Illicit Drug Use among American Secondary School Students, College Students and Young Adults, 1975–1991*. Ann Arbor: The University of Michigan Institute for Social Research; Rockville, Md.: National Institute for Drug Abuse, 1992.

Kaufman, Philip, Marilyn M. McMillen, and Denise Bradby. *Dropout Rates in the United States, 1991*. Washington, D.C.: GPO, 1992.

Kozol, Jonathan. *Savage Inequalities: Children in America's Schools*. New York: Crown Publishers, Inc., 1991.

National Commission on Excellence in Education. *A Nation at Risk*. Portland, Ore.: U.S. Research, Inc., 1993.

"Poverty and Health." *The Washington Post Health Magazine*, July 28, 1992.

Rasell, M. Edith, and Lawrence Mishel. *Shortchanging Education: How U.S. Spending on Grades K–12 Lags Behind Other Industrial Nations*. Washington, D.C.: Economic Policy Institute, 1990.

Research and Policy Committee. *The Unfinished Agenda: A New Vision for Child Development and Education*. New York: The Committee for Economic Development, 1991.

Richman, Louis S. "Struggling to Save Our Kids." *Fortune*, August 10, 1992.

Shapiro, Isaac, and Robert Greenstein. *Selective Prosperity: Increasing Income Disparities since 1977*. Washington, D.C.: Center on Budget and Policy Priorities, 1991.

Snyder, Thomas D., and Charlene M. Hoffman. *Digest of Education Statistics, 1992*. Washington, D.C.: GPO, 1992.

Snyder, Thomas D., editor. *One Hundred and Twenty Years of American Education: A Statistical Portrait*, The Progress of Nations. New York: Gordon Press Publishers, 1993.

Urban Institute. *The Urban Institute Policy and Research Report*. Washington, D.C.: The Urban Institute Press, Winter/Spring 1993.

U.S. Bureau of the Census. *Poverty in the United States: 1992*. Washington, D.C.: Bureau of the Census, 1993.

Walker, John H., Ernest J. Kozmo, and Robert P. Green, Jr. *American Education, Foundations and Policy*. Saint Paul, Minn.: West Publishing Company.

Chapter Four

Abramowitz, Kenneth S. "The Future of Health Care Delivery in America." *Bernstein Research*. Delivered at the National Managed Health Care Congress Conference, April 15, 1993.

American Association of Retired Persons. *The AARP Public Policy Agenda, 1993: Toward a Just and Caring Society*. Washington, D.C.: American Association of Retired Persons, 1993.

Bernheim, D. Douglas., M.D. "Is the Baby Boom Generation Preparing Adequately for Retirement?" Merrill Lynch, Pierce, Fenner and Smith, Inc., 1993.

Caplan, Richard, and John Feffer. *State of the Union, 1994: The Clinton Administration and the Nation in Profile*. Boulder, Col.: Westview Press, 1994.

Day, Jennifer Cheeseman. *Populations of the United States by Age, Sex, Race and Hispanic Origin, 1993–2050*. Washington, D.C.: U.S. Bureau of the Census, 1993.

Dychtwald, Ken, Ph.D. *Age Wave: Choices and Challenges for Our New Future*. New York: Bantam Books, 1990.

Edsall, Thomas Byrne, and Mary D. Edsall. *Chain Reaction: The Impact of Race Rights and Taxes on American Politics*. New York: W. W. Norton and Company, 1991.

Gaylin, William, M.D. "Faulty Diagnosis: Why the Clinton Health Care Plan Won't Work." *Harper's*, October 1993.

Georges, Christopher. "Old Money: Why the AARP Spends as Much Furnishing Its Offices As It Does on Programs to Help the Elderly." *The Washington Monthly*, 1992.

Gerber, Jerry, Janet Wolff, Walter Klures, and Gere Brown. *Lifetrends: The Future of Baby Boomers and Other Aging Americans*. New York: Macmillan Publishing Company, 1989.

Howe, Neil. *Controlling Entitlements: The Argument for Comprehensive "Means-Testing."* Washington, D.C.: National Taxpayers' Union Foundation, 1992.

———. *1991 NTUF Chartbook, Entitlements and the Aging of America*. Washington, D.C.: National Taxpayers' Union Foundation, 1991.

Kaplan, George. "Suppose They Gave an Intergenerational Conflict and Nobody Came." *Kaplan Special Report*, 1991.

Kinsella, Kevin, and Cynthia M. Taeuber. *An Aging World II*. Washington, D.C.: U.S. Bureau of the Census, 1993.

Koitz, David, Gene Falk, and Philip Winters. *CRS Report for Congress:*

Trust Funds and the Federal Deficit. Washington, D.C.: Congressional Research Service, 1990.

Kotlikoff, Larence J. and Jagadeesh Gokhale. "Passing the Generational Buck." *Public Interest,* 1994.

Kuhn, Susan E. "How You Can Afford to Retire Well." *Fortune,* July 26, 1993.

Lamm, Richard D. *Prodigal Parents: The 21st Series.* Boulder: The Center for Public Policy and Contemporary Issues, University of Denver, 1991.

Longman, Philip. *Born to Pay: The New Politics of Aging in America.* Boston: Houghton Mifflin and Company, Inc., 1987.

Melville, Kevin. *The Health Care Crisis: Containing Costs, Expanding Coverage.* Dubuque, Iowa: Kendall/Hunt Publishing Company, 1992.

Peterson, Peter. "Facing Up." *The Atlantic Monthly,* October 1993.

————. "An Immodest Proposal." *Daedalus,* 1992.

Schiff, Irwin A. *The Social Security Swindle.* New York: Freedom Books, 1984.

Smith, Lee. "The Tyranny of America's Old." *Fortune,* 1992.

Steuerle, C. Eugene and Jon M. Bakija. *Retooling Social Security for the 21st Century.* Washington, D.C.: The Urban Institute Press, 1994.

Strauss, William, Neil Howe, and Ian Williams. *Thirteenth Generation: Abort, Retry, Ignore, Fail?* New York: Vintage Books, 1993.

"Trust Funds and the Federal Deficit." *Congressional Research Service.* February 26, 1990.

U.S. Department of Labor. *Outlook: 1990–2005, The Bureau of Labor Statistics Employment Projections.* Washington, D.C.: GPO, 1992.

U.S. Senate Special Committee on Aging. *Aging America: Trends and Projections.* Washington, D.C.: The Federal Council on the Aging and the U.S. Administration on the Aging, 1991.

Williams, Ian. "Let's Kiss That Baby Boom Goodbye." *The Washington Post Magazine,* January 2, 1994.

Chapter Six

Aspin, Les. *Report on the Bottom-up Review.* Washington, D.C.: United States Department of Defense, 1993.

Barnet, Richard J. *The Rockets' Red Glare: When America Goes to War—The Presidents and the People.* New York: Simon and Schuster, Inc., 1990.

Brown, Lester R. *State of the World, 1994: A Worldwatch Institute Report on Progress Toward a Sustainable Society.* New York: W. W. Norton and Company, 1994.

――――. *State of the World, 1993: A Worldwatch Institute Report on Progress Toward a Sustainable Economy.* New York: W. W. Norton and Company, 1993.

Brown, Lester R., Christopher Flavin, and Hal Kane. *Vital Signs: The Trends That Are Shaping Our Future.* New York: W. W. Norton and Company, 1992.

Ehrenhalt, Alan. *The United States of Ambition.* New York: Random House, Inc., 1991.

Felten, Eric. *The Ruling Class: Inside the Imperial Congress.* Washington, D.C.: The Heritage Foundation, 1992.

Greenberg, Jonathan, and William Kistler. *Buying America Back.* Tulsa, Okla.: Council Oak Books, 1992.

Gross, Martin. *A Call for Revolution: How Washington Is Strangling America—and How to Stop It.* New York: Ballantine Books, 1993.

Henry, Lon H. *Congress, America's Privileged Class.* Roseville, Calif.: Prima Publishing, 1994.

Sivard, Ruth Leger. *World Military and Social Expenditures, 1993, 15th Edition.* Washington, D.C.: World Priorities, 1993.

Stern, Philip. *Still the Best Congress Money Can Buy.* Washington, D.C.: Regnery Gateway, 1992.

Taibl, Paul and Steven Kosiak. *An Affordable Long-term Defense.* Washington, D.C.: Defense Budget Project, 1993.

U.S. Arms Control and Disarmament Agency. *World Military Expenditures and Arms Transfers, 1990.* New York: Gordon Press Publishers, 1991.

Weiner, Tim. *Blank Check: The Pentagon's Black Budget.* New York: Warner Books, Inc., 1990.

Wolpe, Bruce C. *Lobbying Congress: How the System Works.* Washington, D.C.: Congressional Quarterly, Inc., 1990.

General

Aaron, Henry J., and Charles Schultze, editors. *Setting Domestic Priorities, What Can Government Do?* Washington, D.C.: The Brookings Institution, 1992.

Clinton, Bill, and Al Gore. *Putting People First: How We Can All Change America*. New York: Times Books, 1992.

Cuomo Commission on Trade and Competitiveness. *A New American Formula for a Strong Economy*. New York: Simon and Schuster, Inc., 1988.

Davis, Kenneth C. *Don't Know Much about History: Everything You Need to Know about American History but Never Learned*. New York: Crown Publishing Company, 1990.

Green, Mark, editor. *Changing America: Blueprints for the New Administration*. New York: Newmarket Press, 1992.

Kennedy, Paul. *Preparing for the Twenty-first Century*. New York: Random House, Inc., 1993.

IV: 100 HARSHEST FACTS ABOUT YOUR FUTURE

A generation of whiners. That's the way the national news media often portray younger Americans. In our defense, many of us point out that the brutal facts speak for themselves. The prospects regarding income, home ownership, job skills, tax rates, and long-term economic opportunities are gloomy. We're not whining. We're realistic, and we're mad.

Not all the critics trash us. John Chancellor, the elder statesman of network news, referred to us on NBC as "the most invisible and possibly the most mistreated generation in American history."

Still the debate rages on. Whiners or Realists? You be the judge.

Here are the 100 harshest facts about your future:

1. Children born in 1994 will face lifetime tax rates of more than 80 percent. (Clinton administration 1994 budget.)

2. A teenager in 1990 was less likely to die of an accident, a cardiovascular disease, or pneumonia than his or her peer in 1960, but more than twice as likely to die by suicide or homicide. (Public Health Service of the United States.)

3. Since the first members of our generation were born (1961), America has experienced a 560 percent increase in violent crime, a 400 percent increase in births to unwed mothers, a tripling in teenage suicide, and a drop of almost 80 points in SAT scores. (*Index of Leading Cultural Indicators*, William Bennett.)

4. Real wages peaked in 1973 and have been declining ever since, yet we work an average of one month more per year than we did two decades ago. (*The Great U-Turn*.)

5. Air pollution costs the U.S. as much as $40 billion annually in health care and lost economic productivity. (Worldwatch State of the World Report.)

6. Each year U.S. factories spew 3 million tons of toxic chemicals into the air, land, and water. That compounds the over one-half billion tons of solid hazardous wastes—we're not talking about your garbage here—that get dumped across the nation for our generation to one day clean up. (*The Gale Environmental Sourcebook*.)

7. Black teenagers are three times more likely to be killed by gun violence than by natural causes. (*Children's Defense Fund Adolescent Fact Book*.)

8. During the last 30 years the number of children living in poverty has increased by nearly 30 percent—with the greatest increase among white kids. (*Vanishing Dreams*.)

9. A monthly investment of $50 for 20 years will only provide for one year of tuition at a public college or university. (*USA Today*.)

10. The total cost to clean up our toxic waste mess is almost three-quarters of a trillion dollars—half the entire U.S. budget for a year. (Worldwatch State of the World Report.)

11. Fifteen percent of all infants born in 1994 will be exposed to illegal drugs while in the womb, and over 100,000 babies are

born with crack addiction. (Fordham University and the Office of National Drug Control.)

12. Since the mid-1970s, poverty among young adults (18 to 34) has gone up by 50 percent—while the median income of under-30 parents fell by a third. (*Vanishing Dreams.*)

13. The median wage for an 18- to 24-year-old man dropped nearly 20 percent during the 1980s—and it continues to decline. (*Vanishing Dreams.*)

14. Half of the nation's uninsured population is under the age of 25. (National Health Survey, 1984.)

15. In 1987, the U.S. released 1.2 million tons of toxic chemicals into our atmosphere, 670,000 tons into our soil, and 250,000 tons into our water. (*International Wildlife* magazine.)

16. In 1970, the Japanese had none of the world market share in dynamic random access memories, a semiconductor device; by 1988, that share had risen to 80 percent. (*Selling Our Security.*)

17. In 1993, AIDS was the top killer of young adults in 64 cities and five states. In addition, the number of people with AIDS worldwide is expected to go from 14 million to 30 million by 2000. (*USA Today.*)

18. Twenty-five percent of all African-American men in their 20s are either in prison, on probation, or on parole. And in the nation's capital, 70 percent of all black men will be arrested at least once before reaching the age of 35. (*Two Nations.*)

19. Each year, 24,000 Americans—on average, 65 each day—are killed with handguns, and we spend over $1 billion annually to treat firearm injuries. (*Handgun Control, Inc.*)

20. Almost half of all Americans between the ages of 21 and 25 lack basic literacy skills, and are unable to balance a check-

book or read a map. (Children's Defense Fund—*State of America's Children 1992.*)

21. One in five Philadelphia teenagers misses school every day. (Monitor Radio.)

22. American teenagers ranked number one in the world in saying they were good at math—and last in a simultaneously administered international math proficiency test. (Educational Testing Service.)

23. A young black man in Harlem, New York, is less likely to live until age 40 than a young man in Bangladesh. (*The New England Journal of Medicine.*)

24. Nearly half of all the new full-time jobs created in the 1980s paid less than $250 a week, or $13,000 a year, below the poverty line for a family of four. (*Fortune* magazine.)

25. According to "moderate projections," between 1995 and 2005 there will be almost half a million more new college graduates a year entering the job market than there will be new jobs. (Bureau of Labor Statistics.)

26. Every day, over 2,500 American children witness the divorce or separation of their parents. Every day, 90 kids are taken from their parents' custody and committed to foster homes. Every day, 13 Americans age 15 to 24 commit suicide, and another 16 are murdered. (*Thirteenth Generation.*)

27. In the last ten years, the number of functionally illiterate 17-year-olds has more than doubled. Today, 7 million teenagers are functionally illiterate. (Children's Defense Fund.)

28. In 1974, the U.S. government declared a health care crisis because we spent 7.5 percent of our gross national product on medical costs. Today we spend twice that much. (*State of the Union,* 1994.)

29. U.S. health care spending has risen from $121 billion in 1961 to a projected $1.3 trillion by 2000. (Congressional Budget Office.)

30. In 1991 the U.S. trailed most industrialized countries in spending on social programs and led in defense spending. (The World Bank.)

31. In an early 1990s report, the government's own accountants found that if current trends continue, federal expenditures will grow from 23 percent of the GNP to 42 percent by 2020, pushing up taxes. (U.S. General Accounting Office.)

32. The elderly (age 65 and up) population will grow 153 percent between now and 2040. (Social Security Administration.)

33. American firms pay twice as much to borrow money and make new investments as do their foreign counterparts. (*U.S. News & World Report.*)

34. The collapse of America's savings and loans will cost taxpayers at least $180 billion. (Congressional Budget Office.)

35. Ninety-five percent of our solid waste is disposed of in almost-filled landfills—and one out of every two of those landfills desperately needs repair so it won't leak. (National Urban League.)

36. Almost two-thirds of the nation's roads need repair. More than 41 percent of our bridges are structurally unsound. (National Urban League.)

37. According to Vice President Al Gore, we are losing species of animals and plants 1000 times faster than at any time in the past 65 million years. (*Earth in the Balance.*)

38. "Federal judges have ordered jails closed and new ones built because the conditions violated the rights of the prisoner. Some of our schools wouldn't pass such scrutiny." (Rep. Dale Kildee, member of the House Education Committee.)

39. America has the largest number of functional illiterates in the industrial world. (Richard Lamm, *Uncompetitive Society.*)

40. The average murderer serves less than seven years because of prison crowding. (U.S. Bureau of Justice Statistics.)

41. Since 1970, arrests for violent crimes by youths have jumped 91 percent. (Office of Juvenile Justice and Delinquency.)

42. The number of guns in America increased from 54 million in 1950 to 201 million in 1990. (Bureau of Justice Statistics.)

43. The Fortune 500 industrial companies employed 3.7 million fewer workers in 1991 than in 1981—a loss of about one job in four. That trend will only worsen into the next century. (*Fortune.*)

44. Today's average, married senior citizen paid $83,852 in Social Security and Medicare taxes. The average senior gets back $308,328. (The Ways and Means Committee.)

45. Only 2.8 percent of German children live in poverty. Over 20 percent of all American kids do. (Pete Peterson, *Facing Up.*)

46. In the last twenty years, income for parents under the age of 30 dropped 28.6 percent, while it rose 28.4 percent for seniors. (1992 census survey.)

47. In the next 35 years, health care spending is expected to eat up twice as much of our economy as it does today. (U.S. Health Care Financing Administration.)

48. The U.S. infant mortality rate is higher than that of 18 other major industrialized countries. (*State of the World's Children*, UNICEF.)

49. We're behind every major country except Hong Kong in average science test scores for 14-year-olds. (International Association for the Evolution of Educational Achievement, 1988.)

50. The U.S. is 17th in public spending on education. (Organization for Economic Cooperation and Development.)

51. "Vital parts of the military equipment that helped win the Gulf War were made in Germany, Japan and other foreign countries," write Martin and Susan Tolchin. "The need to

beg foreign embassies for essential parts was chilling."
(*Selling Our Security*.)

52. There are 3 million homeless people in America—the same
    number as in *all* of Europe. (Coalition for the Homeless,
    1992.)

53. The current average skill level of 21- to 25-year-olds is 40
    percent lower than the skill level that will be required of new
    workers in the year 2000—only six years from today. (The
    Hudson Institute.)

54. The median home price, adjusted for inflation, has jumped
    78 percent since the early 1960s, making ownership out of
    the reach of many young families. (*Forbes*.)

55. In 1975, the U.S. planned on having a high-level nuclear
    waste disposal site operating by 1985. It will not be ready
    until 2010 at best. (Vital Statistics, Worldwatch Institute.)

56. Nearly one in three college graduates between 1990 and
    2005 is expected to take a job that doesn't require a college
    degree—up from 1 in 10 in the 1960s. (*Wall Street Journal*.)

57. "It's hard to see why someone age 68 should automatically
    pay lower taxes than someone age 28 with the same income.
    Yet, that happens." (Robert Samuelson, *Newsweek*.)

58. A 30-year-old man in the early 1970s earned 15 percent
    more than his father did at that age. Today's 30-year-old can
    expect to bring in 25 percent less than his dad did. (*Forbes*.)

59. By 2002, Uncle Sam will have stolen over $1 trillion from the
    Social Security trust fund. (OASDHI 1993.) .

60. Poverty affected 11.1 percent of Americans in 1973 and 14
    percent by the early 1990s. (1992 Census.)

61. "The Great American Job Machine . . . is shifting gears—
    downward. Solid middle-class jobs . . . have been disappear-
    ing in record numbers and are being replaced more often
    than not by lower wage jobs." (*Fortune*.)

62. Since the early 1970s, the poverty rate among under-30 households has doubled. (The Economic Policy Institute.)

63. From 1929 to 1933 (the years of the Great Depression), real income fell by 25 percent. For couples with kids in our generation, it's dropped 30 percent. (*Thirteenth Generation*)

64. Estimated costs of cleaning up the 24,000 contaminated federal nuclear facilities range from $100 billion to $400 billion. (The Environmental Protection Agency.)

65. In 1948, a family of four earning the median income would have paid no income tax and a mere 1 percent to Social Security. By 1955, income tax and Social Security would require 9 percent, and by 1990 the combined tax burden was 25 to 28 percent. (*Boiling Point.*)

66. Baby boomers are saving only about one-third as much as they need. This means their kids will have to finance their retirements. (Merrill Lynch.)

67. From 1981 to 1989, the number of American home-owners between the ages of 25 and 29 declined by 11 percent, while the number of renters in that same age group rose by 16 percent. ("Housing in America," U.S. Department of Commerce, 1992.)

68. Today's 63-year-old will get back roughly $200 for every $100 he or she pays into Social Security. Today's 25-year-old will *lose* over $100 for every $450 paid into Social Security. (The Wyatt Company.)

69. As a share of workers' payroll, the total cost of Social Security and Medicare could climb from 17 percent today to over 50 percent by 2040. (OASDHI, 1992.)

70. Twenty-five percent of full-time workers do not earn enough to rise out of poverty. (U.S. Census Bureau.)

71. The U.S. spends 6 percent of the GNP on the military; Japan spends less than 1 percent. Seventy percent of all U.S.

research and development testing and evaluation goes to the military. (Uncompetitive Society Report.)

72. From 1971 to 1988, only 50 percent of all eligible voters turned out on election day—the worst record of any major democracy. (World Values Survey, January 1987.)

73. America spends more money on health care than any other country—but American males rank 15th in world life expectancy, and females are eighth. (Uncompetitive Society Report.)

74. "There are two kinds of U.S. electronics companies," explains the chairman of the American Electronics Association, "those that are screaming in pain from the Japanese and those that will be screaming in pain."

75. When the national debt hits $6.5 trillion, interest on the debt will gobble up 85 percent of all personal taxes. (*Bankruptcy 1995.*)

76. The average cost in 1990 dollars of attending a private four-year college more than doubled from 1965 to 1990. (U.S. Department of Education.)

77. From the mid-1970s to the late 1980s, the average tuition at a private college as a part of an average family income rose in ratio almost 50 percent. (*USA Today.*)

78. The U.S. spends nearly $1 trillion annually on health care, yet nearly 75 million Americans are either underinsured or completely uninsured. Both Canada and Germany spend 30 to 40 percent less on health care per capita, and both provide universal health care. (*The Washington Monthly.*)

79. Every day, the typical 14-year-old watches three hours of TV and does one hour of homework. Every day, over 2,200 kids drop out of school. Every day, 3,610 teenagers are assaulted, 630 are robbed, and 80 are raped. Every day, 500 adolescents begin using illegal drugs and 1,000 begin drink-

ing alcohol. Every day, 1,000 unwed teenage girls become mothers. (*Thirteenth Generation.*)

80. The president of American Express, Louis Gerstner, Jr., stated, "Forty percent of high school seniors can't name three South American countries. . . . One-third of today's ninth graders can't write a brief summary of a newspaper story. Will [these people] be able to take phone messages from important clients?"

81. Only 66 percent of eighth graders and 77 percent of twelfth graders correctly totaled the cost of soup, burger, fries, and cola on a restaurant menu. (*USA Today.*)

82. Contrast the very different television experiences of a typical boomer born in the late 1940s with a typical 13er born two decades later. By age five, the boomer had seen little or no television; the 13er had seen 5,000 hours' worth, thanks to a parent who probably used TV as a baby-sitter. (*Thirteenth Generation.*)

83. Since 1969, in inflation-adjusted dollars, the average Social Security benefit for a retired worker has risen by 80 percent. Meanwhile, the inflation-adjusted average AFDC benefit for a child in poverty has declined by over 10 percent. (Social Security Administration.)

84. Some 3 million attempted or completed street crimes (assault, rape, robbery, theft) take place on school property annually. One in 20 teachers is assaulted each year. One in five of today's high school students has at one time carried a gun or other weapon to school. That amounts to 32 percent of all boys, 8 percent of all girls. (U.S. Public Health Service.)

85. In his book *Powernomics: Economics and Strategy After the Cold War*, former U.S. trade negotiator Clyde Prestowitz stated, "On a national basis, about 25 percent of our students drop out of high school, consigned to a social and economic scrap heap before they even begin their adult lives.

The U.S. is the only major nation of the world that tolerates such human waste."

86. Each year through the 1980s, 5,000 youths between the ages of 15 and 25 killed themselves. Surveys show that 10 percent of adolescent boys and 18 percent of adolescent girls are willing to admit that they have attempted suicide. "What can one say about a generation 1,000,000 of whom have tried (or will try) to kill themselves before age 30—and 100,000 of whom have succeeded (or will succeed) in their final effort?" (*Thirteenth Generation.*)

87. In 1992, the U.S. spent $24.9 billion to jail 1.3 million prisoners—a per-prisoner cost of $20,072—while we spent $4,000 per public school student. (*Washington Monthly.*)

88. From 1973 to 1990, real median income of U.S. families aged 65 and over went up 39 percent, while it dropped 16 percent for families headed by someone aged 30 or under. (U.S. Bureau of the Census.)

89. In 1979, 74 percent of working Americans under age 25 were earning an hourly wage which—if received full-time and year-round—exceeded the cash poverty level for a family of three. By 1991, that share had fallen to 47 percent. (The Children's Defense Fund.)

90. In the early 1970s, for a typical married couple under age 30, the after-tax cost of owning a first home consumed just 12 percent of income. By the 1990s, the after-tax cost of owning the same house had risen to 29 percent of income. (Joint Center for Housing Studies of Harvard University.)

91. In 1990, a couple in their twenties with one worker, a baby, and $30,000 in income had to pay five times as much tax to the government ($5,055) as the typical retired couple in their late sixties with the same incomes from public and private pensions ($1,073). (Congressional Ways and Means Committee.)

92. Since 1965, juvenile violent-crime arrest rates have tripled. (U.S. Federal Bureau of Investigation.)

93. Among Americans age 25 to 29, the number of homeowners declined by 11 percent from 1981 to 1989, while the number of renters rose by 16 percent. (Housing in America Report.)

94. Given the way things are, it will be much harder for people in our generation to live as comfortably as those in previous generations.

Agree: 65%
Disagree: 33%
(*Time* magazine poll of Americans under 30.)

95. In 1987, Colgate-Palmolive started a program to groom recent college graduates for overseas managerial careers. By the early 1990s, more than 15,000 young people were vying for the 15 slots available each year. (*The Wall Street Journal.*)

96. Number and proportions of persons not covered by health insurance at any time during 1990, by age bracket.

Under Age 18	8.4 million	(24.3%)
Age 18 to 34	14.8 million	(42.8%)
Age 35 to 64	11.1 million	(32.1%)
Age 65 and over	0.3 million	(0.8%)

(U.S. Bureau of the Census)

97. The average 30-year-old home-owner in the 1950s could make the monthly mortgage payment using 14 percent of his income. Today it would take 40 percent. (Frank Levy.)

98. In 1900, the U.S. government consumed less than 9 percent of the gross national product (the nation's total economic output). By 1990, the government was costing almost 40 percent of the gross national product. On a per-capita basis the growth in the cost of government was even greater, going from $1,651 per person in 1900 to over $23,000 in 1990. These statistics are based on real 1990 dollars. (Institute for Policy Innovation.)

99. During every 100 hours on our inner-city streets, three times more young American men lose their lives in gunfire than were young American men killed during 100 hours of Operation Desert Storm. (U.S. Bureau of the Census.)

100. In 1992, handguns were used in the murders of 33 people in Britain, 36 in Sweden, 97 in Switzerland, 128 in Canada, 13 in Australia, 60 in Japan, and 13,220 in the United States. (*The New York Times*.)

ACKNOWLEDGMENTS

This book, and the message it carries, wouldn't have been possible without the help, inspiration, and dedication of many other people.

Special thanks to:

The founding staffers of Lead . . . or Leave—in particular Nick Nyhan, Chris Fuller, Ali Wolf, Jeremy Hartman, Heather McCullough, Justin Kelley, Karen Booth, and Jaimy Chadam—for dedicating what money can't buy—commitment and passion—toward a new vision for our generation.

The enthusiatic Lead . . . or Leave interns—including Sarita, Jeannie, Gary, Meredith, Eddie, Kris, Nisha, Bethany, Tony, Bill, Stu, Caroline, Kirsten and Kristen, Thomas, Kara, Scott, Jaime, Paul, Andrew, and Karen—for working harder than any other interns in Washington. Shari, Sara, Chris, Maria, Mike, and the other phone warriors for their guerrilla grassroots efforts. The Leadership Summit volunteer crew. Norman, for having the courage to believe and to try. And the countless Lead . . . or Leave volunteers across the country. You make this movement possible.

Rafe Sagalyn, our agent, for believing in *Revolution X*, and helping us see that life may look better in black and white, but more often shows up in gray. Nan Graham, our editor at Viking Penguin, for an approach that allowed our book to reflect both our vision and our voice. Courtney Hodell, Nan's associate, for her editorial help (and nearly endless patience). Heide Paddock, who designed the cover, for having creative bursts at just the right time.

Extra special thanks to:

Jon Gallagher, our researcher, for showing up at just the right time—and knowing where to find almost anything. Our Edmunds Street housemates who tolerated a few months of chaos. Friends like Beth and Charles Miller, Paul Tudor Jones, and Richard Dennis. And our families, who've been supportive all along.

Nick, who changed gears in his life, came to D.C., slept on a couch, and lent his vision to help make Lead . . . or Leave what it is today.

Jane, for helping bring our book to life.

Lucy, for your clarity, friendship, and that special way you have of telling the truth.

And finally to Paul Tsongas, who in May of 1992, took our phone call and was willing to stand by our efforts and our generation.

FOR THE BEST IN PAPERBACKS, LOOK FOR THE ⓟ

In every corner of the world, on every subject under the sun, Penguin represents quality and variety—the very best in publishing today.

For complete information about books available from Penguin—including Pelicans, Puffins, Peregrines, and Penguin Classics—and how to order them, write to us at the appropriate address below. Please note that for copyright reasons the selection of books varies from country to country.

In the United Kingdom: For a complete list of books available from Penguin in the U.K., please write to *Dept E.P., Penguin Books Ltd, Harmondsworth, Middlesex, UB7 0DA.*

In the United States: For a complete list of books available from Penguin in the U.S., please write to *Consumer Sales, Penguin USA, P.O. Box 999— Dept. 17109, Bergenfield, New Jersey 07621-0120.* VISA and MasterCard holders call 1-800-253-6476 to order all Penguin titles.

In Canada: For a complete list of books available from Penguin in Canada, please write to *Penguin Books Canada Ltd, 10 Alcorn Avenue, Suite 300, Toronto, Ontario, Canada M4V 3B2.*

In Australia: For a complete list of books available from Penguin in Australia, please write to the *Marketing Department, Penguin Books Ltd, P.O. Box 257, Ringwood, Victoria 3134.*

In New Zealand: For a complete list of books available from Penguin in New Zealand, please write to the *Marketing Department, Penguin Books (NZ) Ltd, Private Bag, Takapuna, Auckland 9.*

In India: For a complete list of books available from Penguin, please write to *Penguin Overseas Ltd, 706 Eros Apartments, 56 Nehru Place, New Delhi, 110019.*

In Holland: For a complete list of books available from Penguin in Holland, please write to *Penguin Books Nederland B.V., Postbus 195, NL-1380AD Weesp, Netherlands.*

In Germany: For a complete list of books available from Penguin, please write to *Penguin Books Ltd, Friedrichstrasse 10-12, D-6000 Frankfurt Main 1, Federal Republic of Germany.*

In Spain: For a complete list of books available from Penguin in Spain, please write to *Longman, Penguin España, Calle San Nicolas 15, E-28013 Madrid, Spain.*

In Japan: For a complete list of books available from Penguin in Japan, please write to *Longman Penguin Japan Co Ltd, Yamaguchi Building, 2-12-9 Kanda Jimbocho, Chiyoda-Ku, Tokyo 101, Japan.*